Samsung® Galaxy S8™

by Bill Hughes

LONGWOOD PUBLIC LIBRARY

Samsung® Galaxy S8™ For Dummies®

Published by: **John Wiley & Sons, Inc.,** 111 River Street, Hoboken, NJ 07030-5774, www.wiley.com

Copyright © 2017 by John Wiley & Sons, Inc., Hoboken, New Jersey

Published simultaneously in Canada

No part of this publication may be reproduced, stored in a retrieval system or transmitted in any form or by any means, electronic, mechanical, photocopying, recording, scanning or otherwise, except as permitted under Sections 107 or 108 of the 1976 United States Copyright Act, without the prior written permission of the Publisher. Requests to the Publisher for permission should be addressed to the Permissions Department, John Wiley & Sons, Inc., 111 River Street, Hoboken, NJ 07030, (201) 748-6011, fax (201) 748-6008, or online at http://www.wiley.com/go/permissions.

Trademarks: Wiley, For Dummies, the Dummies Man logo, Dummies.com, Making Everything Easier, and related trade dress are trademarks or registered trademarks of John Wiley & Sons, Inc. and may not be used without written permission. Samsung and Galaxy S8 are trademarks or registered trademarks of Samsung Electronics Company, Ltd. All other trademarks are the property of their respective owners. John Wiley & Sons, Inc. is not associated with any product or vendor mentioned in this book.

LIMIT OF LIABILITY/DISCLAIMER OF WARRANTY: THE PUBLISHER AND THE AUTHOR MAKE NO REPRESENTATIONS OR WARRANTIES WITH RESPECT TO THE ACCURACY OR COMPLETENESS OF THE CONTENTS OF THIS WORK AND SPECIFICALLY DISCLAIM ALL WARRANTIES, INCLUDING WITHOUT LIMITATION WARRANTIES OF FITNESS FOR A PARTICULAR PURPOSE. NO WARRANTY MAY BE CREATED OR EXTENDED BY SALES OR PROMOTIONAL MATERIALS. THE ADVICE AND STRATEGIES CONTAINED HEREIN MAY NOT BE SUITABLE FOR EVERY SITUATION. THIS WORK IS SOLD WITH THE UNDERSTANDING THAT THE PUBLISHER IS NOT ENGAGED IN RENDERING LEGAL, ACCOUNTING, OR OTHER PROFESSIONAL SERVICES. IF PROFESSIONAL ASSISTANCE IS REQUIRED, THE SERVICES OF A COMPETENT PROFESSIONAL PERSON SHOULD BE SOUGHT. NEITHER THE PUBLISHER NOR THE AUTHOR SHALL BE LIABLE FOR DAMAGES ARISING HEREFROM. THE FACT THAT AN ORGANIZATION OR WEBSITE IS REFERRED TO IN THIS WORK AS A CITATION AND/OR A POTENTIAL SOURCE OF FURTHER INFORMATION DOES NOT MEAN THAT THE AUTHOR OR THE PUBLISHER ENDORSES THE INFORMATION THE ORGANIZATION OR WEBSITE MAY PROVIDE OR RECOMMENDATIONS IT MAY MAKE. FURTHER, READERS SHOULD BE AWARE THAT INTERNET WEBSITES LISTED IN THIS WORK MAY HAVE CHANGED OR DISAPPEARED BETWEEN WHEN THIS WORK WAS WRITTEN AND WHEN IT IS READ.

For general information on our other products and services, please contact our Customer Care Department within the U.S. at 877-762-2974, outside the U.S. at 317-572-3993, or fax 317-572-4002. For technical support, please visit https://hub.wiley.com/community/support/dummies.

Wiley publishes in a variety of print and electronic formats and by print-on-demand. Some material included with standard print versions of this book may not be included in e-books or in print-on-demand. If this book refers to media such as a CD or DVD that is not included in the version you purchased, you may download this material at http://booksupport.wiley.com. For more information about Wiley products, visit www.wiley.com.

Library of Congress Control Number: 2017943307

ISBN 978-1-119-38223-2 (pbk); ISBN 978-1-119-38227-0 (ebk); ISBN 978-1-119-38224-9 (ebk)

Manufactured in the United States of America

10 9 8 7 6 5 4 3

Contents at a Glance

Table of Contents

Introduction

The Samsung Galaxy S8 and S8+ are powerful smartphones, perhaps the most powerful mobile phones ever sold. As of the publication of this book, the Galaxy S8s are the standard against which all other Android-based phones are measured.

Each cellular carrier offers a slightly customized version of the Galaxy S8 line-up. Some phones from cellular carriers come out of the box with preloaded applications, games, or files. Most come with accessories, such as a corded headset; others don't. This book doesn't dwell on these kinds of differences.

The name for each network is different, these phones are largely the same. (At least one marketing person at each cellular carrier is cringing as you read this.) This similarity allows me to write this book in a way that covers the common capabilities.

At a more core level, these phones are built for high-speed wireless communications. The cellular carriers have spent kajillions upgrading their networks to offer more coverage and better data speeds than their competition. Again, this book doesn't dwell on these differences in network technology because they don't really make much difference. (Again, at least one engineering person at each cellular carrier is cringing as you read this.)

Similarly, most of the capabilities of the Galaxy S8+, with its bigger screen, and the Galaxy S8 are identical. When there is an important distinction between the S8 and the S8+, I will mention it. Otherwise, I will just call the phone the Galaxy S8.

I assume that you already have a Galaxy S8, and I just hope that you have good coverage where you spend more of your time with your phone. If so, you'll be fine. If not, you need to switch to another network; otherwise, the experience with your phone will be frustrating. I would advise you to return your phone to that carrier and buy your Galaxy S8 at another cellular carrier. As long as you have good cellular data coverage, owning a Samsung Galaxy S8 will be an exciting experience!

First, in much the same way that different brands of PCs are all based on the Microsoft Windows operating system, all Galaxy S phones use the Google Android platform. The good news is that the Android platform has proven to be widely popular, even more successful than Google originally expected when it first announced Android in November 2007. More people are using Android-based phones, and more third parties are writing applications. This is good news because it offers you more options for applications (more on this in Chapter 8 on the Play Store, where you buy applications).

In addition, all Galaxy S8 phones use a powerful graphics processor, employ Samsung's Super AMOLED touchscreen, and are covered in Corning's Gorilla Glass. The superior screen experience differentiates this product line from other Android phones. Because of these enhanced capabilities, you can navigate around the screen with multi-touch screen gestures instead of the hierarchical menus found on lesser Android phones. Plus, the videos look stunning from many angles.

Smartphones are getting smarter all the time, and the Galaxy S8 is one of the smartest. However, just because you've used a smartphone in the past doesn't mean you should expect to use your new Galaxy S8 without a bit of guidance.

You may not be familiar with using a multi-touch screen, and your new phone offers a lot of capabilities that you may or may not be familiar with. There used to be a physical button on the front to bring you back to the Home screen. It's no longer a physical button; instead, it's now software based. It would be unfortunate to find out from a kid in the neighborhood that the phone you've been carrying around for several months could solve a problem you've been having because you were never told that the solution was in your pocket the whole time.

In fact, Samsung is proud of the usability of its entire Galaxy line-up — and proud that the user's manual is really just a quick start guide. You can find lots of instructions on the web. However, you have to know what you don't know to get what you want unless you plan to view every tutorial.

That's where this book comes in. This book is a hands-on guide to getting the most out of your Galaxy S8.

About This Book

This book is a reference — you don't have to read it from beginning to end to get all you need out of it. The information is clearly organized and easy to access. You don't need thick glasses to understand this book. This book helps you figure out what you want to do — and then tells you how to do it in plain English.

Within this book, you may note that some web addresses break across two lines of text. If you're reading this book in print and want to visit one of these web pages, simply key in the web address exactly as it's noted in the text, pretending as though the line break doesn't exist. If you're reading this as an e-book, you've got it easy — just click the web address to be taken directly to the web page.

Foolish Assumptions

You know what they say about assuming, so I don't do much of it in this book. But I do make a few assumptions about you:

>> **You have a Galaxy S8 phone.** You may be thinking about buying a Galaxy S8 phone, but my money's on your already owning one. After all, getting your hands on the phone is the best part!

>> **You're not totally new to mobile phones.** You know that your Galaxy S8 phone is capable of doing more than the average phone, and you're eager to find out what your phone can do.

>> **You've used a computer.** You don't have to be a computer expert, but you at least know how to check your email and surf the web.

Icons Used in This Book

Throughout this book, I used *icons* (little pictures in the margin) to draw your attention to various types of information. Here's a key to what those icons mean:

This whole book is like one big series of tips. When I share especially useful tips and tricks, I mark them with the Tip icon.

This book is a reference, which means you don't have to commit it to memory — there is no test at the end. But once in a while, I do tell you things that are so important that I think you should remember them, and when I do, I mark them with the Remember icon.

Whenever you may do something that could cause a major headache, I warn you with the, er, Warning icon.

These sections provide a little more information than is necessary to use your phone. The hope is that these sections convey extra knowledge to help you understand what is going on when things go wrong, or at least differently than you might have expected.

Beyond the Book

In addition to what you're reading right now, this product also comes with a free access-anywhere Cheat Sheet. To get to this Cheat Sheet, simply go to www. dummies.com and type **Samsung Galaxy S8 For Dummies Cheat Sheet** in the Search box.

Where to Go from Here

You don't have to read this book from cover to cover. You can skip around as you like. For example, if you need the basics on calling, texting, and emailing, turn to Part 2. To discover more about photos, games, and apps, go to Part 4.

Many readers are already somewhat familiar with smartphones and won't need the basic information found in Parts 1 and 2. A reasonably astute mobile phone user can figure out how to use the phone, text, and data capabilities. Parts 1 and 2 are not for those readers. For them, I recommend skipping ahead to the chapters in Parts 3 through 6.

Former iPhone users, on the other hand, are a special case. (First, welcome to the world of Android!) The reality is that the iPhone and Galaxy S series have very similar capabilities, but these functions are just done in slightly different ways and emphasize different approaches to the similar problems. iPhone users, don't worry if you find that this book spends a fair amount of time explaining capabilities with which you're familiar. You can read through those chapters quickly, focus on the *how* instead of the description of *what*, and bypass potential frustration.

Current Samsung Galaxy S7 users are also a special case. The Samsung Galaxy S8 is very similar to the Galaxy S7 in many ways. Galaxy S8 operates mostly like the S7, but has improvements in usability, power consumption, and performance. If you're comfortable with the Galaxy S7 and now have a Galaxy S8, Chapters 15 and beyond would be of interest to you.

The majority of readers of this book are actually very astute and get the fact that this book covers the basics of using the Samsung Galaxy S8. A subset of readers complain in Internet reviews that a *For Dummies* book is too basic. If you do this, people will know that you did not read the title. Be sure to read the title and avoid public embarrassment.

1

Getting Started with the Samsung Galaxy S8

Review the capabilities of cellphones and what sets smartphones apart.

Navigate your phone for the first time.

Turn off your phone and manage sleep mode.

Make sense of mobile data technology.

» **Understanding what sets smartphones apart**

» **Mapping out what makes Samsung Galaxy S8 phones so cool**

» **Getting you prepared to enjoy your phone**

Chapter **1**

Exploring What You Can Do with Your Phone

Whether you want just the basics from a mobile phone (make and take phone calls, customize your ringtone, take some pictures, maybe use a Bluetooth headset) or you want your phone to be always by your side (a tool for multiple uses throughout your day), you can make that happen. In this chapter, I outline all the things your Samsung Galaxy S8 can do — from the basics to what makes Galaxy S8 phones different from the rest.

Discovering the Basics of Your Phone

All mobile phones on the market today include basic functions, and even some entry-level phones are a little more sophisticated. Of course, Samsung includes all basic functions on the Galaxy S8 model. In addition to making and taking calls (see Chapter 3) and sending and receiving texts (see Chapter 4), the Galaxy S8 sports the following basic features:

>> **12MP digital camera:** This resolution is more than enough for posting good-quality images on the Internet and even having 8 x 10-inch prints made. There is also a front-facing camera with 8MP that is useful for videoconference calls and selfies.

>> **Ringtones:** You can replace the standard ringtone with custom ringtones that you download to your phone. You also can specify different rings for different numbers.

>> **Bluetooth:** The Galaxy S8 phone supports stereo and standard Bluetooth devices. (See Chapter 3 for more on Bluetooth.)

>> **High-resolution screen:** The Galaxy S8 phone offers one of the highest-resolution touchscreens on the market (2,960 x 1,440 pixels).

>> **Capacitive touchscreen:** The Galaxy S8 phone offers a very slick touchscreen that's sensitive enough to allow you to interact with the screen accurately, but not so sensitive that it's hard to manage. In addition, it has an optional setting that steps up the sensitivity for special circumstances, like when you want to use one hand!

Taking Your Phone to the Next Level: The Smartphone Features

In addition to the basic capabilities of any entry-level phone, the Galaxy S8, which is based on the popular Android platform for mobile devices, has capabilities associated with other smartphones, such as the Apple iPhone:

>> **Internet access:** Access websites through a web browser on your phone.

>> **Photos:** The Galaxy S8 comes with a very intelligent camera that has millions of combinations of settings, filters, and resolutions and also has the capability to manage photos.

>> **Wireless email:** Send and receive email from your phone.

>> **Multimedia:** Play music and videos on your phone.

>> **Contact Manager:** The Galaxy S8 lets you take shortcuts that save you from having to enter someone's ten-digit number each time you want to call or text a friend. In fact, the Contact Manager can track all the numbers that an individual might have, store an email address and photo for the person, and

synchronize with the program you use for managing contacts on both your personal and work PCs!

>> **Digital camcorder:** The Galaxy S8 comes with a built-in digital camcorder that records live video at a resolution that you can set, including 4K/UHD (ultra-high definition, which is just now available on the newest televisions).

>> **Mapping and directions:** The Galaxy S8 uses GPS (Global Positioning System) along with other complementary positioning systems to tell you where you are, find local services that you need, and give you directions to where you want to go.

>> **Fitness information:** The Galaxy S8 automatically tracks important health information within the phone and with external sensors.

>> **Business applications:** The Galaxy S8 can keep you productive while you're away from the office.

I go into each of these capabilities in greater detail in the following sections.

Internet access

Until a few years ago, the only way to access the Internet when you were away from a desk was with a laptop. Smartphones are a great alternative to laptops because they're small, convenient, and ready to launch their web browsers right away. Even more important, when you have a smartphone, you can access the Internet wherever you are — whether Wi-Fi is available or not.

The drawback to smartphones, however, is that their screen size is smaller than that of even the most basic laptop. On the Galaxy S8 phone, you can use the standard version of a website if you want. You can pinch and stretch your way to get the information you want. (See Chapter 2 for more information on pinching and stretching. For more information on accessing the Internet from your Galaxy S8 phone, turn to Chapter 7.)

To make things a bit easier, many popular websites offer an easier-to-use app that you can download and install on your phone. This is discussed in detail in Chapter 8. Essentially, the website reformats the information from the site so that it's easier to read and navigate in the mobile environment. Figure 1-1 compares a regular website with the app version of that website.

Photos

The image application on your phone helps you use the digital camera on your Galaxy S8 phone to its full potential. (It would almost make sense to call the Samsung Galaxy S8 a smartcamera with a built-in phone!)

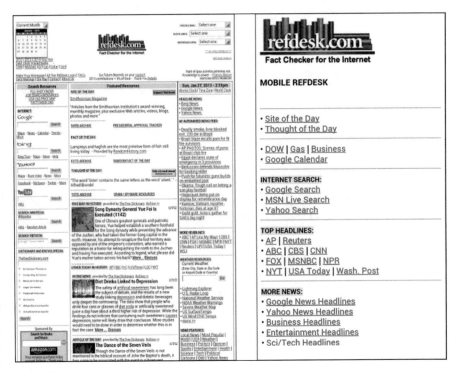

FIGURE 1-1:
A website
and the app
version of the
main site.

Studies have found that cellphone users tend to snap a bunch of pictures within the first month of phone usage. After that, the photos sit on the phone (instead of being downloaded to a computer), and the picture-taking rate drops dramatically.

The Galaxy S8 image management application is different. You can integrate your camera images into your home photo library, as well as photo-sharing sites such as Google Photos and Flickr, with minimal effort.

For more on how to use the Photo applications, turn to Chapter 9.

Wireless email

On your Galaxy S8 smartphone, you can access your business and personal email accounts, reading and sending email messages on the go. Depending on your email system, you might be able to sync so that when you delete an email on your phone, the email is deleted on your computer at the same time so that you don't have to read the same messages on your phone and your computer.

Chapter 5 covers setting up your business and personal email accounts.

Multimedia

Some smartphones allow you to play music and videos on your phone in place of a dedicated MP3 or video player. On the Galaxy S8, you can use the applications that come with the phone, or you can download applications that offer these capabilities from the Play Store.

Chapter 12 covers how to use the multimedia services with your Galaxy S8 phone.

An intelligent agent

Chapter 14 explores how to use Samsung's intelligent agent called Bixby. You simply ask Bixby to take care of things for you, such as update an appointment or check for prices and Bixby will go off and do it.

Customizing Your Phone with Games and Applications

Application developers — large and small — are working on the Android platform to offer a variety of applications and games for the Galaxy S8 phone. Compared to most of the other smartphone platforms, Google imposes fewer restrictions on application developers regarding what's allowable. This freedom to develop resonates with many developers — resulting in a bonanza of application development on this platform.

As of this writing, almost two million applications are available from Google's Play Store. For more information about downloading games and applications, turn to Chapter 8.

Downloading games

Chapter 10 of this book is for gamers. Although your phone comes with a few general-interest games, you can find a whole wide world of games for every skill and taste. In Chapter 10, I give you all the information you need to set up different gaming experiences. Whether you prefer stand-alone games or multiplayer games, you can set up your Galaxy S8 phone to get what you need.

Downloading applications

Your phone comes with some very nice applications, but these might not take you as far as you want to go. You might also have some special interests, such as philately or stargazing, that neither Samsung nor your carrier felt would be of sufficient general interest to include on the phone. (Can you imagine?)

Your phone also comes with preloaded *widgets*, which are smaller applications that serve particular purposes, such as retrieving particular stock quotes or telling you how your phone's battery is feeling today. Widgets reside on the extended Home screen and are instantly available.

Buying applications allows you to get additional capabilities quickly, easily, and inexpensively. Ultimately, these make your phone, which is already a reflection of who you are, even more personal as you add more capabilities.

What's cool about the Android platform

The Samsung Galaxy S8 is the top-of-the-line Android phone. That means you can run any application developed for an Android phone to its full capability. This is significant because one of the founding principles behind the Android platform is to create an environment where application developers can be as creative as possible without an oppressive organization dictating what can and cannot be sold (as long as it's within the law, of course). This creative elbow room has inspired many of the best application developers to go with Android first.

In addition, Android is designed to run multiple applications at once. Other smartphone platforms have added this capability, but Android is designed to let you to jump quickly among the multiple apps that you're running — which makes your smartphone experience that much smoother.

TAKE A DEEP BREATH

You don't have to rush to implement every feature of your Galaxy S8 phone the very first day you get it. Instead, pick one capability at a time. Digest it, enjoy it, and then tackle the next one.

I recommend starting with setting up your email and social accounts, but that's just me.

No matter how you tackle the process of setting up your Galaxy S8 phone, it'll take some time. If you try to cram it all in on the first day, you'll turn what should be fun into drudgery.

The good news is that you own the book that takes you through the process. You can do a chapter or two at a time.

WHAT IF I DIDN'T GET MY PHONE FROM A CELLULAR COMPANY?

With a few exceptions, such as an "unlocked" GSM phone, each phone is associated with a particular cellular company. (In this context, a *locked* phone can work only on its original carrier.) Maybe you bought a secondhand phone on eBay, or you got a phone from a friend who didn't want his anymore. If you didn't get your phone directly from a cellular provider, you will need to figure out which provider the phone is associated with and get a service plan from that company. Some Galaxy S8 phones sold in the United States all have the cellular company's logo on the phone printed on the front. That makes it easy to know under which carrier a phone will operate.

If there's no logo on the front, you'll have to figure out which cellular carrier it can work with. The quickest way is to take the phone to any cellular store; the folks there know how to figure it out.

To narrow down the possibilities on your own, you need to do some investigation. Take off the back of the phone to find the plate with the model and serial number for the phone. If you see IMEI on the plate, the phone is based on a technology called Global System for Mobile (GSM); it'll work with AT&T, T-Mobile, MetroPCS (or all of them). If you see ESN on the plate, the phone will work with Verizon, Sprint, or US Cellular.

Surviving Unboxing Day

When you turn on your phone the first time, it will ask you a series of ten questions and preferences to configure it. Frankly, they are trying to make this book unnecessary and put me out of business. The nerve!

The good folks at Samsung are well-intentioned, but not every customer who owns a Samsung Galaxy S8 knows, from day one, whether he or she wants a Samsung account, what's a good name for the phone, or what the purpose of a cloud service, such as Dropbox, is and how it would be used.

You can relax. I'll help you answer these questions — or, when appropriate, refer you to the chapter in this book that helps you come up with your answer.

On the other hand, if your phone is already set up, you probably took a guess or skipped some questions. Maybe now you're rethinking some of your choices. No problem. You can go back and change any answer you gave and get your phone to behave the way you want.

The following are the kinds of questions you may be asked. These questions may come in this order, but they may not. They typically include the following:

» **Language/Accessibility:** This option lets you select your language. The default is English for phones sold within the United States. Also, the phone has some special capabilities for individuals with disabilities. If you have a disability and think you might benefit, take a look at these options. They have really tried to make this phone as usable as possible for as many folks as possible.

» **Wi-Fi:** Your phone automatically starts scanning for a Wi-Fi connection. You can always use the cellular connection when you are in cellular coverage, but if there is a Wi-Fi connection available, your phone will try to use this first. It is probably cheaper and may be faster than the cellular.

At the same time, you may not want your phone to connect to the Wi-Fi access point with the best signal. It could be that the strongest signal is a fee-based service, whereas the next best signal is free. In any case, this page scans the available options and presents them to you.

» **Date and Time:** This is easy. The default setting is to use the time and date that comes from the cellular network and the date and time format is the U.S. style. Just tap on the next button and move on. This date and time from the cellular network is the most accurate information you'll get, and you don't need to do anything other than be within cellular coverage now and again. If you prefer non-U.S. formatting, such as a 24-hour clock or day/month/year formatting, you can change your phone any way you want.

» **Sign up for a Samsung Account:** Go ahead and sign up for an account. The Samsung account offers you some nice things to help you get your phone back should you lose it. All you need is an account name, such as an email account, and a password.

TIP

When you buy a Galaxy S8 smartphone, you are now a customer of multiple companies! These include Samsung for the phone hardware, Google for the phone operating system (Android), and the wireless carrier that provides the cellular service. Plus, if you bought the phone through a phone retailer, such as Best Buy, it is in the mix as well. All of them want to make you happy, which is a good thing for the most part. The only downside is that they want to know who you are so that they can provide you with more services. Don't worry. You control how much they offer you.

» **Google Account Sign-up:** *Google account* means an email account where the address ends in @gmail.com. If you already have an account on Gmail, enter your user ID and password here. If you don't have a Gmail account, I suggest waiting until you read Chapter 5. I highly recommend that you create a Gmail account, but there are some considerations on selecting a good name. If you are game, pick a name for your Gmail account now. Otherwise, it can wait until you read Chapter 5.

» **Location Options:** Your phone knowing your location and providing it to an application can be sensitive issue.

If you're really worried about privacy and security, tap the green check marks on the screen and then tap the button that says Next. Selecting these options prevents applications from knowing where you are. (This choice also prevents you from getting directions and a large number of cool capabilities that are built into applications.) The only folks who'll know your location will be the 911 dispatchers if you dial them.

If you're worried about your security but want to take advantage of some of the cool capabilities built into your phone, tap the right arrow key to move forward. Remember, you can choose on a case-by-case basis whether to share your location. (I cover this issue in Chapter 8.)

» **Phone Ownership:** This screen asks you to enter your first and last name. Go ahead and put in your real name. If you want to know more, read Chapter 5.

» **Cloud Services:** The chances are that you will be offered the option to sign up for a cloud service where you can back up your phone and get access to a gazillion MB of free storage. This can be a tricky decision. You could sign up for every cloud service that comes along. Then you need to remember where you stored that critical file. You could sign up for one, and you may miss a nice capability that is available on another. You could have one cloud service for work and another for personal. Here is what I recommend: Sign up for whatever is the cloud service your phone offers during this initial setup process if you do not already have one. You will see what it is later. If you are happy with a cloud service you already have, such as Dropbox or OneDrive, chances are, they will have all the services you need for you and your phone. You can link your Galaxy S8 to this service by downloading the necessary app (which I cover how to do in Chapter 8).

» **Learn about Key Features:** If you think you don't need this book, go ahead and take this tour of all the new things you can do. If you think you might need this book in any way, shape, or form, tap the Next button. This screen is for setting up the coolest and the most sophisticated capabilities of the phone. I cover many of them in this book. For now, skip this to get to the last screen.

>> **Device Name:** When this screen comes up, you'll see a text box that has the model name. You can keep this name for your phone, or you can choose to personalize it a bit. For example, you can change it to "Bill's Galaxy S8" or "Indy at 425-555-1234." The purpose of this name is for connecting to a local data network, as when you're pairing to a Bluetooth device. If this last sentence made no sense to you, don't worry about it. (I go over all of this in Chapter 3.) Tap Finish. In a moment, you see the Home screen, as shown in Figure 1-2.

FIGURE 1-2: The Home screen for the Samsung Galaxy S8.

Chapter **2**

Beginning at the Beginning

I n this chapter, I fill you in on the basics of using your new Samsung Galaxy S8. You start by turning on your phone. (I told you I was covering the basics!) I guide you through charging your phone and getting the most out of your phone's battery. Stick with me for a basic tour of your phone's buttons and other features. Then I end by telling you how to turn off your phone or put it in "sleep" mode.

TIP

Unless you're new to mobile phones in general — and smartphones in particular — you might want to skip this chapter. If the term "smartphone" is foreign to you, you probably haven't used one before, and reading this chapter won't hurt. And, just so you know, a *smartphone* is just a mobile phone on which you can download and run applications that are better than what comes preloaded on a phone right out of the box.

First Things First: Turning On Your Phone

When you open the box of your new phone, the packaging will present you with your phone, wrapped in plastic, readily accessible. If you haven't already, take the phone out of the box and remove any protective covering material on the screen. (There is no need to keep the plastic. It is not an effective screen protector!)

First things first. The Power button is on the right side of the phone. You can see where in Figure 2-1. Press the Power button for a second and see whether it vibrates and the screen lights up. Hopefully, your phone arrived with enough electrical charge that you won't have to plug it into an outlet right away. You can enjoy your new phone for the first day without having to charge it.

FIGURE 2-1: The Power button on the Galaxy S8.

The phones that you get at the stores of most cellular carriers usually come with the battery installed, partially charged, and registered with the network.

REMEMBER

If the screen does light up, don't hold the Power button too long, or the phone might turn off.

If the phone screen doesn't light up (rats!), you need to charge the battery. Here's the rub: It's important to fully charge the battery for 24 hours, or at least overnight, so that it will last as long as possible. That means that you have to wait to use your beautiful new phone. Sorry.

THE NITTY-GRITTY OF HOW YOUR PHONE WORKS

TECHNICAL STUFF

As soon as you turn on your phone, several things happen. As the phone is powering up, it begins transmitting information to (and receiving information from) nearby cellular towers. The first information exchanged includes your phone's electronic serial number. Every cellphone has its own unique serial number built into the hardware of the phone; the serial number in current-generation cellphones can't be duplicated or used by any other phone.

This electronic serial number is also called an International Mobile Equipment Identity (IMEI) number. It is 14 or 15 digits long. Cellular equipment is fine with long numbers. We mere mortals have enough trouble remembering 10-digit numbers, even with the hack of having only a limited number of area codes. To help us out, you and I get to use the shorter number and the cellular equipment happily keeps track of the 10-digit and the 14/15-digit numbers and shows us only what we can handle.

It doesn't matter to the phone or the cellular tower if you're near your home when you turn on your phone — and that's the joy of mobile phones. All cellular networks have agreements that allow you to use cellular networks in other parts of the country and, sometimes, around the world.

That said, a call outside your cellular provider's own network may be expensive. Within the United States, many service plans allow you to pay the same rate if you use your phone anywhere in the United States to call anywhere in the United States. If you travel outside the United States, even to Canada, you might end up paying through the nose. *Remember:* Before you leave on a trip, check with your cellular carrier about your rates. Even if you travel internationally only a few times yearly, a different service plan may work better for you. Your cellular carrier can fill you in on your options.

Charging Your Phone and Managing Battery Life

In the package when you buy your phone, you find a two-piece battery charger (cable and the transformer), as shown in Figure 2-2.

FIGURE 2-2:
The transformer and USB cable for charging your phone.

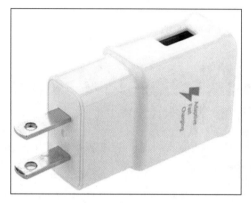
Wall Charger

USB-A/USB-C Cable

The cable has two ends: one end that plugs into the phone, and the other that's a standard rectangular USB connector. The phone end is a small connector called a *USB-C* that is used on many Samsung devices and is the standard for charging cellphones and other small electronics — and for connecting them to computers.

TIP

One cool thing you will notice about the USB-C connector is that you can insert it either side up. The older, rectangular USB-A connector probably drove you crazy because it wouldn't go in if you had the plug upside down. You still have that problem with the wall charger and cable, but you won't have the problem with the cable and phone!

To charge the phone, you have two choices:

>> Plug the transformer into a wall socket and then plug the cable's USB plug into the USB receptacle in the transformer.

>> Plug the USB on the cable into a USB port on your PC.

Then you plug the small end of the cable into the phone. The port is on the bottom of the phone. You will see that the top is a little smaller than the bottom. It's a trapezoid with rounded edges. Orient the plug with the hole in the phone and make sure that you push the little metal plug all the way in.

REMEMBER

It doesn't really matter in what order you plug in things. However, if you use the USB port on a PC, the PC needs to be powered on for the phone to charge.

TIP

Your phone will charge faster with a Samsung wall charger that has Adaptive Fast Charging on it. When the wall charger, or car charger has Adaptive Fast Charging, it knows if the phone is getting too warm and slow down the speed of charging. Because the charging speed can slow down, it can go faster the rest of the time.

If your phone is off when you're charging the battery, an image of a battery appears onscreen for a moment. The green portion of the battery indicates the amount of charge within the battery. You can get the image to reappear with a quick press of the Power button. This image tells you the status of the battery without your having to turn on the phone.

If your phone is on, you see a small battery icon at the top of the screen showing how much charge is in the phone's battery. When the battery in the phone is fully charged, it vibrates to let you know that it's done charging and that you should unplug the phone and charger.

It takes only a few hours to go from a dead battery to a fully charged battery. Other than the first time you charge the phone, you don't need to wait for the battery to be fully charged. You can partially recharge and run if you want.

TIP

You'll hear all kinds of "battery lore" left over from earlier battery technologies. For example, lithium–ion (Li–ion) batteries in your S8 don't have a "memory" (a bad thing for a battery) as nickel–cadmium (NiCad) batteries did. That means that you don't have to make sure that the battery fully discharges before you recharge it.

In addition to the transformer and USB cable that come with the phone, you have other optional charging tools:

- **USB travel charger:** If you already have a USB travel charger, you can leave the transformer at home. This accessory will run you about $15. You still need your cable, although any USB-to-micro-USB cable should work.

- **Car charger:** You can buy a charger with a USB port that plugs into the power socket/cigarette lighter in a car. This is convenient if you spend a lot of time in your car. The list price is $30, but you can get the real Samsung car charger for less at some online stores.

- **Portable external charger:** You can buy a portable external charger with a micro-USB port that you can use to recharge your phone without having to plug into the power socket or cigarette lighter in a car. You charge this gizmo before your travel and connect it only when the charge in your phone starts to get low. These usually involve re-chargeable batteries, but some of these products use photovoltaic cells to transform light into power. As long as there is a USB port (the female part of the USB), all you need is your cable. These chargers can cost from $30 to $100 on up. See some options in Figure 2-3.

>> **Wireless charger:** This option is slick. You simply put your phone on a charging mat or in a cradle, and the phone battery will start charging! Your Galaxy S8 uses the widely adopted Qi standard (pronounced *chee*). This option saves you from having to plug and unplug your phone.

FIGURE 2-3: Some portable external charging options.

WARNING

Ideally, use Samsung chargers or chargers from reputable manufacturers or retailers. The power specifications for USB ports are standardized. Reputable manufactures comply with these standards, but less reputable manufacturers might not. Cheap USB chargers physically fit the USB end of the cable that goes to your phone. However, Li-ion batteries are sensitive to voltage. There are many, many creative options available outside the store where you bought your phone, but avoid the allure of low price.

WARNING

Be aware that the conditions that make for a good charge with a photocell also tend to make for high heat. It will do you little good to have a beautifully function-ing charger and a dead phone.

Most of the chargers out there are either for the Apple iPhone and have an Apple Lightning connector or have a micro–USB connector. As you know, your phone has a USB-C connector. A micro USB will not work with a USB-C connector. You either need to get a cable that has a USB-C connector or use an adapter that will allow you to connect micro USB to a USB-C connector. Figure 2-4 shows the micro USB to USB-C adapter next to a dime for a size comparison.

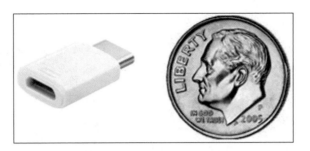

FIGURE 2-4:
The micro
USB to USB-C
adapter.

TECHNICAL
STUFF

ONLY YOU CAN PREVENT PHONE FIRES

The Galaxy S8 uses lithium-ion (Li-ion) batteries. As the name implies, these batteries are based upon the element lithium (Li). Lithium works really well for cellphone batteries because it's very light.

The problem is that if lithium gets too hot, it burns. Lithium can catch fire at a relatively modest 180°F, and then burn like crazy at 1,100°F. By comparison, dry firewood won't ignite until 451°F, and will then burn at 1,100°F. In other words, lithium burns just as hot as a campfire, but it ignites at a much lower temperature.

To make things safe, battery makers and cellphone manufacturers implement all kinds of sneaky and imaginative methods of removing the heat from around the lithium battery. In addition, your phone invisibly monitors temperatures and takes steps to ensure that it doesn't get too hot. This all works so well and seamlessly that you probably didn't even notice this was happening in your earlier phones and other gizmos that use Li-ion technology.

So, here's the big problem: If things start going wrong with Lithium-ion batteries, many of the sneaky and imaginative methods used to remove the heat begin to fail. The fancy term for what happens next is *thermal runaway*. When thermal runaway happens in a device with a Li-ion battery, one of two things happens:

- The guts of the phone will bubble and melt.

- The battery will burst into flames, throwing sparks for several feet in all directions.

So, what should you do and, perhaps more important, what should you *not* do? If your phone has started to burn, the best possible solution is to dunk it in a glass, bucket, or toilet full of water. If you can't find something to dunk it in, you can throw water on the phone to stop the fire. Water both cools the lithium and prevents oxygen from getting to the flame. I know: Getting your phone wet goes against all your instincts, but once a phone has started bubbling, all your texts and photos have already been lost. Prevent further damage and use water to put out the fire.

(continued)

(continued)

If you don't have water handy, and you're somewhere outside, in a parking lot or on a sidewalk away from people, you can set the phone on the ground, get far away from it, and call 911. Stand far back from the phone. It could explode. For obvious reasons, putting out the fire by dunking the phone in water or dousing it with water is best.

Smothering the phone with a blanket or dirt won't work. Even if you get the fire stopped momentarily with these methods, the battery is likely to start burning again because it's still too hot. A fire extinguisher with anything other than water or a liquid will also not work well. As with a blanket or dirt, the battery stays hot, and when oxygen reaches it, the lithium will simply reignite.

You might think that if water is good at cooling off a Li-ion fire, a pile of ice would be better. Unfortunately, you would be wrong. Check out this video from the Federal Aviation Administration that shows some battery fires: `https://youtu.be/vS6KA_Si-m8`. It shows that a huge pile of ice, which would do wonders to stop a campfire, cools the battery too slowly, and the darn things burns anyway. Go figure.

INCREASING YOUR CHARGING KNOWLEDGE

There are so many charging options out there these days, it can be confusing. My simple advice is to use a USB-C cable from Samsung that has Adaptive Fast Charging. The next best choice is a name-brand charger that has USB-C. Some well-meaning "friends" may try to lead you astray and try something else. Do not allow yourself to be fooled.

The following figure shows some of the options that are out in the market right now. The USB-C is on the left. The ones to the right will not work with your phone. Buying these would be a waste of money unless you plan to use the adapter. Otherwise, these won't fit in the receptacle on your phone.

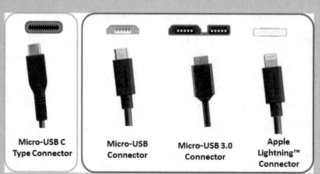

Enlarged Connector Front View

Connector Side View

Micro-USB C Type Connector | Micro-USB Connector | Micro-USB 3.0 Connector | Apple Lightning™ Connector

The first option is the micro-USB. This is what is used on the Galaxy S6, the S7, and many phones from other manufacturers.

The second option is the micro-USB 3.0. The front view of the micro-USB 3.0 connector looks like the micro-USB connector front view with a rectangle welded on to the right. Frankly, it kinda looks silly, which is why it never really caught on. Samsung used it on the Galaxy S5, which is why you might see it in some stores.

The third option is the Apple Lighting cable. This is unlike the others because the connectors are visible rather than being protected by a metal shroud. The best thing about it is that it costs more, as you can see in the figure that shows car charges from Ventev (one of those reputable suppliers I have told you about).

Ventev dashport r2340c charger
with Micro USB Cable $29.99

Ventev dashport r2340c charger w/
Apple Lightning™ Cable $34.99

Images courtesy of Ventev

The same product has a $5 premium for the Apple connector.

Navigating the Galaxy S8

Galaxy S8 phone devices differ from many other mobile phones in design: They have significantly fewer hardware buttons (physical buttons on the phone). They rely much more heavily on software buttons that appear onscreen.

In this section, I guide you through your phone's buttons.

The phone's hardware buttons

Samsung has reduced the number of hardware buttons on the Galaxy S8. There are only three: the Power button, the Volume button, and the Bixby button. Before you get too far into using your phone, orient yourself to be sure that you're looking at the correct side of the phone. When I refer to the *left* or *right* of the phone, I'm assuming a vertical orientation (meaning you're not holding the phone sideways) and that you're looking at the phone's screen.

The Power button

The Power button (refer to Figure 2-1) is on right side of the phone, toward the top when you hold it in vertical orientation.

In addition to powering up the phone, pressing the Power button puts the device into sleep mode if you press it for a moment while the phone is On. *Sleep mode* shuts off the screen and suspends most running applications.

The phone automatically goes into sleep mode after about 30 seconds of inactivity to save power, but you might want to do this manually when you put away your phone. The Super AMOLED (Active-Matrix Organic Light-Emitting Diode) screen on your Samsung Galaxy S8 is cool, but it also uses a lot of power.

REMEMBER

Don't confuse sleep mode with powering off. Because the screen is the biggest user of power on your phone, having the screen go blank saves battery life. The phone is still alert to any incoming calls; when someone calls, the screen automatically lights up.

The Volume button(s)

Technically, there are two Volume buttons: one to increase the volume, and the other to lower it. Their locations are shown in Figure 2-5.

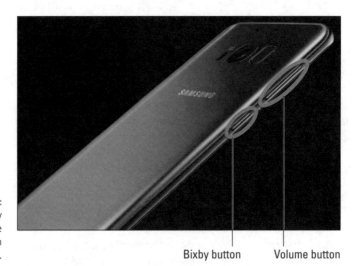

FIGURE 2-5:
The Galaxy
S8 Volume
buttons on
the left.

Bixby button   Volume button

The Volume buttons control the volume of all the audio sources on the phone, including

>> The phone ringer for when a call comes in (ringtone)

>> The notifications that occur only when you're not talking on the phone, such as the optional ping that lets you know you've received a text or email

>> The phone headset when you're talking on the phone

>> The volume from the digital music and video player (media)

The volume controls are aware of the context; they can tell which volume you're changing. For example, if you're listening to music, adjusting volume raises or lowers the music volume, but leaves the ringer and phone-earpiece volumes unchanged.

The Volume buttons are complementary to software settings you can make within the applications. For example, you can open the music-player software and turn up the volume on the appropriate screen. Then you can use the hardware buttons to turn down the volume, and you'll see the volume setting on the screen go down.

Another option is to go to a settings screen and set the volume levels for each scenario. Here's how to do that:

1. **From the Home screen, press either Volume button.**

You can press it either up or down. Doing so brings up the screen shown in Figure 2-6.

If you press the volume up or down, the ring tone gets louder or softer. Hold off on this tweak for now and go to the next step.

2. **From this screen, tap the arrow down in the upper-right corner.**

Tapping it brings up the screen shown in Figure 2-7.

3. **From the screen shown in Figure 2-7, set the volume at the desired setting.**

You can adjust the volume of any setting by placing your finger on the dot on the slider image. The dot will get bigger; you can slide it to the left to lower this particular volume setting or to the right to raise it.

FIGURE 2-6:
The ringer
volume
pop-up.

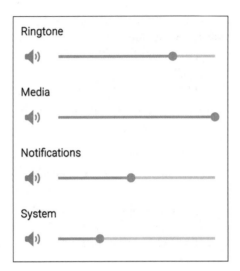

FIGURE 2-7:
The All Volume
Settings
pop-up.

The Bixby button

The Bixby button on the phone is shown in Figure 2-5. It's below the volume buttons. Bixby is an app from Samsung that is an *intelligent agent* (IA). It's like Siri on
the iPhone. I cover Bixby in greater detail in Chapter 14. It's cool, but it still needs
some work. The plan is that you can launch this app by pressing the Bixby button
twice. For now, it will bring you to the Bixby screen.

The touchscreen

To cram all the information that you need onto one screen, Samsung takes the
modern approach to screen layout. You'll want to become familiar with several
finger-navigation motions used to work with your screen.

Before diving in, though, here's a small list of terms you need to know:

- » **Icon:** An *icon* is a little image. Tapping an icon launches an application or
  performs some function, such as making a telephone call.

- » **Button:** A *button* on a touchscreen is meant to look like a three-dimensional
  button that you would push on, say, a telephone. Buttons are typically labeled
  to tell you what they do when you tap them. For example, you'll see buttons
  labeled Save or Send.

- » **Hyperlink:** Sometimes called a *link* for short, a *hyperlink* is text that performs
  some function when you tap it. Usually text is lifeless. If you tap a word and it
  does nothing, then it's just text. If you tap a word and it launches a website or
  causes a screen to pop up, it's a hyperlink.

>> **Thumbnail:** A *thumbnail* is a small, low-resolution version of a larger, high-resolution picture stored somewhere else.

With this background, it's time to discuss the motions you'll be using on the touchscreen.

WARNING

You need to clean the touchscreen glass from time to time. The glass on your phone is Gorilla Glass (made by Corning) — the toughest stuff available to protect against breakage. Use a soft cloth or microfiber to get fingerprints off. You can even wipe the touchscreen on your clothes. However, never use a paper towel! Over time, glass is no match for the fibers in the humble paper towel.

Tap

Often, you just tap the screen to make things happen (as when you launch an app) or select options. Think of a *tap* as a single mouse click on a computer screen. A tap is simply a touch on the screen, much like using a touchscreen at a retail kiosk. Figure 2-8 shows what the tap motion should look like.

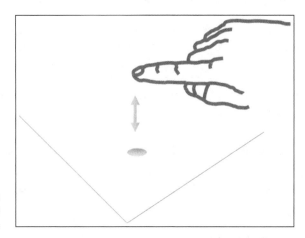

FIGURE 2-8: The tap motion.

One difference between a mouse click on a computer and a tap on a Galaxy S8 phone is that a single tap launches applications on the phone in the same way that a double-click of the mouse launches an application on a computer.

TIP

A tap is different from press and hold (see the next section). If you leave your finger on the screen for more than an instant, the phone thinks you want to do something other than launch an application.

Press and hold

Press and hold, as the name implies, involves putting your finger on an icon on the screen and leaving it there for more than a second. What happens when you leave your finger on an icon depends upon the situation.

For example, when you press and hold on an application on the Home screen (the screen that comes up after you turn on the phone), a garbage-can icon appears onscreen. This is to remove that icon from that screen. And when you press and hold an application icon from the list of applications, the phone assumes that you want to copy that application to your Home screen. Don't worry if these distinctions might not make sense yet. The point is that you should be familiar with holding and pressing — and that it's different from tapping.

TIP

You don't need to tap or press and hold very hard for the phone to know that you want it to do something. Neither do you need to worry about breaking the glass, even by pressing on it very hard. If you hold the phone in one hand and tap with the other, you'll be fine. I suppose you might break the glass on the phone if you put it on the floor and press up into a one-fingered handstand. I don't recommend that, but if you do try it, please post the video on YouTube.

WARNING

On average, a person calls 911 about once every year. Usually, you call 911 because of a stressful situation. Like every phone, the Samsung Galaxy S8 has a special stress sensor that causes it to lock up when you need it most. Okay, not really, but it seems that way. When you're stressed, it's easy to think that you're tapping when you're actually pressing and holding. Be aware of this tendency and remember to *tap.*

Moving around the screen or to the next screen

Additional finger motions help you move around the screens and to adjust the scaling for images that you want on the screen. Mastering these motions is important to getting the most from your phone.

The first step is navigating the screen to access what's not visible onscreen. Think of this as navigating a regular computer screen, where you use a horizontal scroll bar to access information to the right or left of what's visible on your monitor, or a vertical scroll bar to move you up and down on a screen.

The same concept works on your phone. To overcome the practical realities of screen size on a phone that will fit into your pocket, the Galaxy S8 phone uses a *panorama* screen layout, meaning that you keep scrolling left or right (or maybe up and down) to access different screens.

In a nutshell, although the full width of a screen is accessible, only the part bounded by the physical screen of the Galaxy S8 phone is visible on the display. Depending upon the circumstances, you have several ways to get to information not visible on the active screen. These actions include drag, flicks, pinch and stretch, and double taps. I cover all these gestures in the following sections.

Drag

The simplest finger motion on the phone is the *drag.* You place your finger on a point on the screen and then drag the image with your finger. Then you lift your finger. Figure 2-9 shows what the motion looks like.

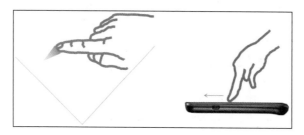

FIGURE 2-9:
The drag motion for controlled movement.

Dragging allows you to move slowly around the panorama. This motion is like clicking a scroll bar and moving it slowly.

Flick

To move quickly around the panorama, you can *flick* the screen to move in the direction of your flick (see Figure 2-10).

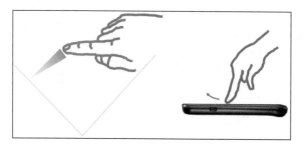

FIGURE 2-10:
Use a flick motion for faster movement.

Better control of this motion comes with practice. In general, the faster the flick, the more the panorama moves. However, some screens (such as the extended Home screen) move only one screen to the right or left, no matter how fast you flick.

Pinch and stretch

Some screens allow you to change the scale of images you view on your screen. When this feature is active, the Zoom options change the magnification of the area on the screen. You can zoom out to see more features at a smaller size or zoom in to see more detail at a larger size.

To zoom out, you put two fingers (apart) on the screen and pull them together to pinch the image. Make sure you're centered on the spot that you want to see in more detail. The pinch motion is shows in Figure 2-11.

FIGURE 2-11:
Use the pinch motion to zoom out.

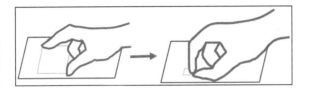

The opposite motion is to zoom in. This involves the stretch motion, as shown in Figure 2-12. You place two fingers (close together) and stretch them apart.

FIGURE 2-12:
Use the stretch motion to zoom in.

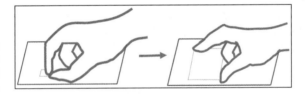

Double tap

The *double tap* (shown in Figure 2-13) just means tapping the same button area on the screen twice in rapid succession. You use the double tap to jump between a zoomed-in and a zoomed-out image to get you back to the previous resolution. This option saves you frustration in getting back to a familiar perspective.

REMEMBER

When you double tap, time the taps so that the phone doesn't interpret them as two separate taps. With a little practice, you'll master the timing of the second tap.

The extended Home screen

The Home screen is the first screen you see when the phone is done with setting up. Additional screens off to the right and left. make up the extended Home screen. They can be seen as a panorama in Figure 2-14.

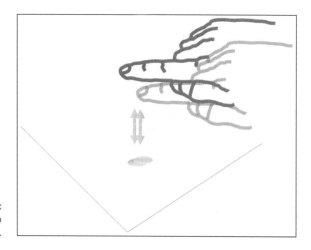

FIGURE 2-13:
The double-tap
motion.

Home Screen

FIGURE 2-14:
The Galaxy
S8 phone
panorama
display of
the extended
Home screen.

At any given moment, you see only one screen at a time. You navigate among the screen by flicking to the right and left. The Home button, which we describe in more detail in the next section, will always bring you back to the Home screen.

The extended Home screen is where you can organize icons and other functions to best make the phone convenient for you. Out of the box, Samsung and your cellular carrier have worked together to create a starting point for you. Beyond that, though, you have lots of ways you can customize your Home screens for easy access to the things that are most important to you. Much of the book covers all the things that the phone can do, but a recurring theme is how to put your favorite capabilities on your Home screen, if you wish.

To start, check out the layout of the Home screen and how it relates to other areas of the phone. Knowing these areas is important for basic navigation.

Figure 2-15 shows a typical Home screen and highlights three important areas on the phone:

>> **The notification area:** This part of the screen presents you with small icons that let you know if something important is up, like battery life or a coupon from McDonald's.

>> **The primary shortcuts:** These five icons remain stationary as you move across the Home screen. If you notice in Figure 2-15, these have been determined by Samsung and your cellular carrier to be the five most important applications on your phone and are on all the screens.

>> **The Function keys:** These three keys control essential phone functions, regardless of what else is going on at the moment with the phone.

TIP

There are a series of dots just above the primary shortcuts on the extended Home screen. You may also notice that one of the dots isn't just a dot — it's a little house. That is the "home" Home screen. The brightest dot indicates where you are among the screens. You can navigate among screens by dragging the screen to the left or right. This moves you one screen at a time. You can also jump multiple screens by tapping on the dot that corresponds to the screen number you want to see or by dragging the dots to the screen you want to see. The following sections give you more detail on each area.

Using the Home button

One of the significant changes Samsung has implemented with the Galaxy S8 is the "invisible" Home button. In past versions of the Galaxy S Phones and Notes, it has been a physical button on the bottom of the front screen. To offer more screen real estate, the S8 makes it a software-based button on the bottom in the center of the function keys.

The Home button (see Figure 2-16) is very important because it brings you back to the Home screen from wherever you are in an application. If you're working on applications and feel like you're helplessly lost, don't worry. Press the Home button, close your eyes, click your heels together three times, and think to yourself, "There's no place like home," and you will be brought back to the Home screen.

Notification area

App Shortcuts

Google Search
Engine with
Voice Recognition

Primary Shortcuts

Function Keys

FIGURE 2-15:
Important
areas on the
Galaxy S8
phone and
Home screen.

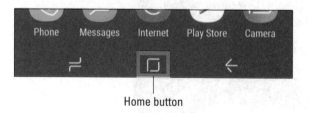

Home button

FIGURE 2-16:
The Galaxy S8
Home button
on the front.

TIP

You don't really need to do all that other stuff after pressing the Home button. Just pressing the Home button does the trick.

Adding shortcuts to the Home screen

You have a lot of screen real estate where you can put icons of your favorite applications and widgets (refer to Figure 2-14). (*Widgets* are small apps that take care of simple functions, like displaying time or the status of your battery.) You can add shortcuts to the apps and to these widgets to your Home screen by following these steps:

1. **From the extended Home screen page where there is some space for the icon of an app, swipe your finger upward on the screen.**

   This brings up a directory of all the apps you currently have on the phone. The page shown in Figure 2-17 shows just one page. The number of apps and pages for their icons is practically unlimited. (I cover how to add new apps in Chapter 8.)

2. **Press and hold the icon of the app you want to add.**

   The screen with the app icons fades, and the extended home page with the space for the icon appears with the icon under your finger.

3. **Move the icon to where you want it to be on the Home screen page and release.**

Done.

FIGURE 2-17:
An Apps page.

Taking away or moving shortcuts

Say that you put the shortcut on the wrong spot. No problem. Press and hold the icon. The screen grays out except for your icon. It looks something like Figure 2-18, except the icon you pressed is in full color under your finger.

FIGURE 2-18: The extended Home screen in repositioning mode.

You then drag the icon to the place on the screen you want it to reside and release. Taking a shortcut off your Home screen is simple: Press and hold the icon on the screen. In a moment, you see the grayed out home page. Drag the doomed shortcut to the garbage can, and off it goes to its maker.

It's gone, but if you made a mistake, you can get it back easily enough. To re-create it, simply go back to the App Menu key and follow the process again.

The notification area and screen

The notification area is located at the top of the phone (refer to Figure 2-15). Here, you see little status icons. Maybe you received a text or an email, or you'll see an application needs some tending to.

Think of the notification area as a special email inbox where your carrier (or even the phone itself) can give you important information about what's happening with your phone. These little icons at the top tell you the condition of the different radio systems on your phone: The number of bars shown gives you an indication of signal strength, and usually the phone will also tell you what kind of mobile data speed you're getting – such as 3G or 4G.

You could take the time to learn the meanings of all the little icons that might come up, but that would take you a while. A more convenient option is to touch the notification area and pull it down, as shown in Figure 2-19.

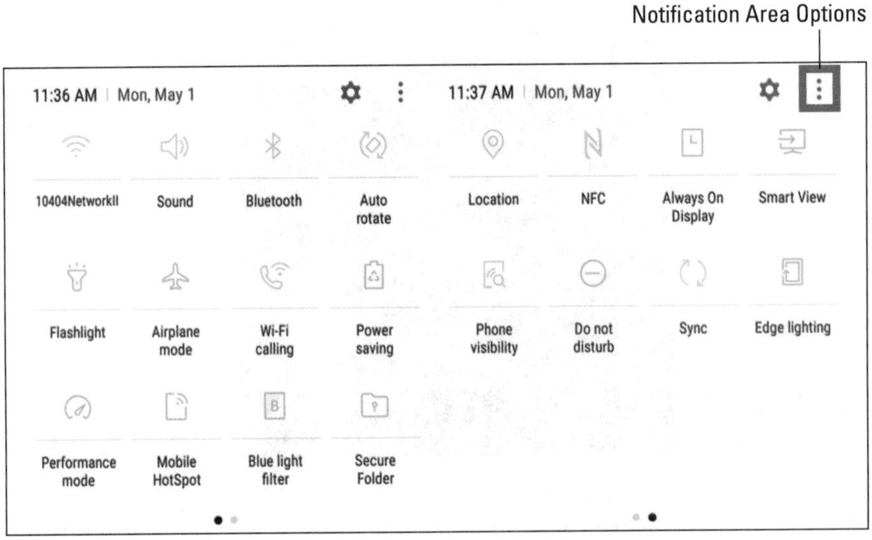

Notification Area Options

11:36 AM Mon, May 1				11:37 AM Mon, May 1			
10404NetworkII	Sound	Bluetooth	Auto rotate	Location	NFC	Always On Display	Smart View
Flashlight	Airplane mode	Wi-Fi calling	Power saving	Phone visibility	Do not disturb	Sync	Edge lighting
Performance mode	Mobile HotSpot	Blue light filter	Secure Folder				

FIGURE 2-19: Notification area pull down.

The rest of the screen is written so that you can understand what's going on and what, if anything, you're expected to do — for example, if you see that you have connected to the Wi-Fi access point you intended.

When you're finished reading the notifications, you slide your finger back up to the top. If this screen gets too full, you can clear it by tapping the Clear button. You can also clear notifications one at a time by touching each one and swiping it to the side.

If you want a shortcut to control some key phone capabilities, you can tap one of these icons. For example, if you want to turn off Wi-Fi, you could just tap the Wi-Fi icon. This would save you from having to get in to Settings to do the same thing.

If you want to add more of these, simply tap the three vertical dots highlighted in Figure 2-19 to see your notification area options. These are seen in Figure 2-20, although you may have slightly different choices on your phone.

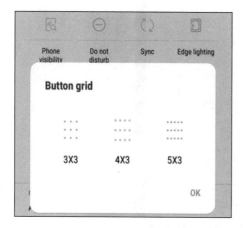

FIGURE 2-20:
Notification
area options.

For example, many people find the Flashlight capability to be handy. If it is not already there when you pull down the notifications screen, see whether it is among the options. If it is, press and hold on the flashlight icon. Then drag it to the top. The other icons scatter, and then you release it. You turn on the flashlight by tapping it. Try it and see.

The Device Function keys

At the bottom of the screen are three important buttons: the Device Function keys. They're always present for you to navigate your phone even though the backlight might switch off to hide their presence. Whatever else you're doing on the phone, these buttons can take over. I talk about the Home button earlier in this chapter. The other buttons are equally cool.

Recent Apps button

The button to the left of the Home button is the Recent Apps button. Tapping the button brings up a list of the open apps. This is handy to navigate between running apps. Figure 2-21 shows a typical screen of recent apps.

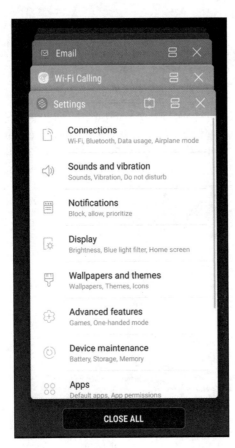

FIGURE 2-21:
Recent Apps
screen.

You can scroll among the open apps by flicking up or down. You can jump to one of these apps by tapping somewhere on the image. You can also shut down one of the apps by tapping the x on the upper-right corner. You can shut them all down by tapping the link at the bottom that says Close All.

TIP

The Device Function keys are cool because they light up when you're touching them or the screen, but fade away the rest of the time.

The Back button

The Back button on your phone is similar to the Back button in a web browser: It takes you back one screen.

As you start navigating through the screens on your phone, tapping the Back button takes you back to the previous screen. If you keep tapping the Back button, you'll eventually return to the Home screen.

The keyboard

The screen of the Galaxy S8 phone is important, but you'll still probably spend more time on the keyboard entering data on the QWERTY keyboard.

Using the software keyboard

The software keyboard automatically pops up when the application detects a need for user text input. The keyboard, shown in Figure 2-22, appears at the bottom of the screen.

FIGURE 2-22:
Use the software keyboard to enter data.

Using Swype

Some Galaxy S8 phones come with an enhanced data-entering capability called Swype. This option may have been preloaded on your phone. If not, you can download it from the Google Play Store. With a little practice, it can dramatically speed your ability to type fast on your phone.

Here's how Swype works: Instead of tapping each discrete key on the keyboard, you leave your finger on the screen and swipe from key to key. The Swype application figures out the words you're wanting to type, including inserting the spaces automatically.

If you like Swype, you can use it anytime you're entering data. If you don't care for it, you can just tap your letters. It's all up to you!

Using voice recognition

The third option for a keyboard is . . . no keyboard at all! Galaxy S8 phones come with voice recognition as an option. It's very easy and works surprisingly well. In most spots where you have an option to enter text, you see a small version of the microphone icon shown in Figure 2-23.

FIGURE 2-23:
The voice
recognition
icon.

Just tap this icon and say what you would have typed. You see the phone thinking for a second, and then a screen tells you that it is listening. Go ahead and start talking. When you're done, you can tap the Done button or just be quiet and wait. Within a few seconds, you'll read what you just said!

The orientation of the phone

Earlier in this chapter where I discuss the Power button, I refer to the phone being in vertical orientation (so that the phone is tall and narrow). It can also be used in the *landscape* orientation (sideways, or so that the phone is short and wide). The phone senses in which direction you're holding it and orients the screen to make it easier for you to view.

REMEMBER

The phone makes its orientation known to the application, but not all applications are designed to change their inherent display. That nuance is left to the writers of the application. For example, your phone can play videos. However, the video player application that comes with your phone shows video in landscape mode only.

In addition, the phone can sense when you're holding it to your ear. When it senses that it's held in this position, it shuts off the screen. You need not be concerned that you'll accidentally "chin-dial" a number in Botswana.

Going to Sleep Mode/Turning Off the Phone

You can leave your phone on every minute until you're ready to upgrade to the newest Galaxy S8 phone in a few years, but that would use up your battery in no time. Instead, put your idle phone in sleep mode to save battery power. *Note:* Your phone goes into sleep mode automatically after 30 seconds of inactivity on the screen.

TIP

You can adjust the sleep time out for a longer duration, which I cover in Chapter 16. Or you can manually put the phone in sleep mode by pressing the Power button for just a moment.

Sometimes it's best to simply shut down the phone if you aren't going to use it for several days or more. To shut down the phone completely, simply press and hold the Power button for a few seconds. The following options appear:

>> **Power Off:** Shut down the phone completely.

>> **Restart:** The Android operating system is stable. Well, mostly stable. Sometimes you may want to reboot it because it starts acting quirky. Tap the restart option and see whether that solves the problem.

>> **Emergency Mode:** This is an interesting option. Once you have agreed to some terms and conditions, your phone will go into hibernation, but it can come back to life quickly if you feel you need to dial 911. Before you can use this option, you need to agree to some of the limitations.

Good night!

2

Communicating with Other People

Chapter **3**

Calling People

A t its essence, any cellphone — no matter how fancy or smart — exists to make phone calls. The good news is that making and receiving phone calls on your Galaxy S8 is easy.

In this chapter, I show you not only how to make a call, but also how to use your call list to keep track of your calls. And don't skip the section on using your phone for emergencies.

Finally, if you're like many people, you're never doing just one thing at a time, and a Bluetooth headset can make it easier for you to talk on the phone while driving and getting directions, checking email, wrangling kids and dogs, or just plain living life. In this chapter, I show you how to hook up your phone to a Bluetooth headset so that you can make and receive phone calls hands-free.

Making Calls

After your phone is on and you're connected to your cellular carrier (see Chapters 1 and 2), you can make a phone call. It all starts from the Home screen. Along the bottom of the screen, above the Device Function keys, are five icons, which are the *primary shortcuts* (see Figure 3-1). The primary shortcuts on your phone may differ slightly, but in this case, from left to right, they are

- » Phone

- » Messages

- » Internet

- » Play Store

- » Camera

FIGURE 3-1:
The primary
shortcuts on
the Home
screen.

To make a call, follow these steps:

1. **From the Home screen, tap the Phone icon.**

   You will see a screen like the one shown in Figure 3-2. This screen shows any calls you have made or received, such as the one from your carrier to confirm that you phone has been set up correctly.

2. **Tap the Dial Pad icon.**

   This icon is a green circle with little white dots that symbolize the touch pad on a regular landline phone.

3. **Tap the telephone number you want to call.**

   The Keypad screen (see Figure 3-3) appears. This looks like a full-sized version of a touch pad on a regular landline phone. (If you have not made or received any calls at all, tapping the Phone icon takes you right to the Keypad screen.)

   Don't be alarmed if you don't hear a dial tone. Smartphones don't connect to a network until after you dial your number and tap Send. At this point, a dial tone would be pointless.

   TIP

   For long distance calls while in the United States, you don't need to dial 1 before the area code — just dial the area code and then the seven-digit phone number. Similarly, you can include the 1 and the area code for local calls. On the other hand, if you're traveling internationally, you need to include the 1 — and be prepared for international roaming charges!

   In Chapter 6, you can read about how to make a phone call through your contacts.

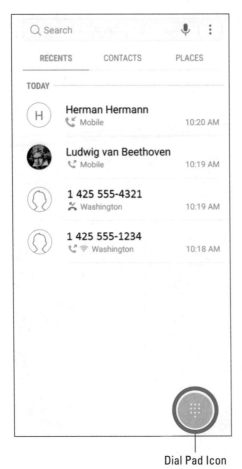

FIGURE 3-2:
The Main
screen for the
phone.

Dial Pad Icon

4. **Tap the green phone button at the bottom of the screen to place the call.**

The screen changes to the screen shown in Figure 3-4. You have a chance to verify you dialed the person you intended.

Within a few seconds, you should hear the phone ringing at the other end or a busy signal. From then on, it is like a regular phone call.

5. **When you're done with your call, tap the red phone button at the bottom of the screen.**

The call is disconnected.

Without Telephone Number | With Telephone Number

FIGURE 3-3:
Dial the num-
ber from the
Keypad screen.

If the other party answers the phone, you have a few options available to you by tapping on the correct icon/hyperlink on the screen, including

>> Put the call on hold

>> Add another call to have a three-way conversation

>> Increase the volume

>> Switch on a Bluetooth device (see the section "Syncing a Bluetooth Headset," later in this chapter)

>> Turn on the phone's speaker

>> Bring up the keypad to enter numbers

>> Mute the microphone on the phone

You can do any or all of these, or you can just enjoy talking on the phone.

FIGURE 3-4:
Dialing screen.

If the call doesn't go through, either the cellular coverage where you are is insufficient, or your phone got switched to Airplane mode, which shuts off all the radios in the phone. (It's possible, of course, that your cellular carrier let you out the door without having set you up for service, but that's pretty unlikely!)

Check the notification section at the top of the screen. If there are no connection-strength bars, try moving to another location. If you see a small airplane silhouette, bring down the notification screen (see how in Chapter 2) and tap the plane icon to turn off Airplane mode.

TIP

If you pull down the notification screen and you don't see the green silhouette of an airplane, scroll the green or gray icons to the left. This icon may be off the page. Alternatively, tap the icon with the boxes in the upper-right corner, and you will see all the notification icons.

Answering Calls

Receiving a call is even easier than making a call. When someone calls you, caller ID information appears in a pop-up screen. Figure 3-5 shows some screen options for an incoming call.

Full Screen Incoming call

Partial Screen Incoming call

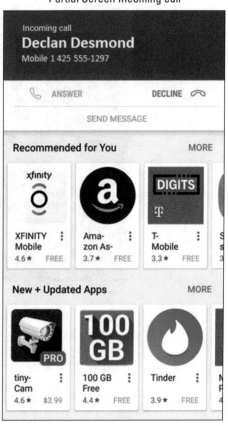

FIGURE 3-5: Possible screens when you're receiving a call.

If you aren't doing anything with the phone at that moment, it will present you with the full screen. If you're using an app, it will give you a pop-up screen, as shown in the image on the right. To answer the call, tap or slide the green phone button. To not answer a call, you can simply ignore the ringing, or you can tap or slide the red phone button. The ringing stops immediately, and in either case, the call goes to voicemail.

TIP

In Part 4, I fill you in on some exciting options that you can enable (or not) when you get a call. For example, you can specify a unique ringtone for a particular number, or have an image of the caller pop up (if you save your contacts to your phone).

Regardless of what you were doing on the phone at that moment — such as listening to music or playing a game — the answer pop-up screen can appear. Any active application, including music or video, is suspended until the call is over.

REMEMBER

For callers to leave you messages, you must set up your voicemail. If you haven't yet set up your voicemail, the caller will hear a recorded message saying that your voicemail account isn't yet set up. Some cellular carriers can set up voicemail for you when you activate the account and get the phone; others require you to set up voicemail on your own. Ask how voicemail works at your carrier store or look for instructions in the manual included with your phone.

The answer and reject icons are pretty standard on any cellular phone. However, your Galaxy S8 is no standard phone. There is a third option, and what happens depends on your individual phone. In addition to the standard options of answer or reject, you have one more option — to reject *and* send the caller a text message. As your caller is sent to your voicemail, you also can immediately send the caller a text message that acknowledges the call.

Some of the typical canned messages that you can send are

>> Sorry, I'm busy. Call back later.

>> I'm in a meeting.

>> I'll call you back.

>> I'm at the movie theater.

>> I'm in class.

You tap the message that applies. The message is sent as a text right away, which alerts the caller that you're not ignoring him — it's just that you can't talk right now. Nice touch.

You can also create and store your own message, like "Go away and leave me alone," or "Whatever I am doing is more important than talking to you." You could also be polite. To create your own canned message, tap Compose new message and type away. It's then stored on your phone for when you need it.

REMEMBER

The caller has to be able to receive text messages on the phone used to make the call. This feature doesn't work if your caller is calling from a landline or a cellphone that can't receive texts.

Keeping Track of Your Calls: The Call List

One of the nice features of cellular phones is that the phone keeps a record of the calls that you've made and received. Sure, you might have caller ID on your landline at home or work, but most landline phones don't keep track of whom you called. Cellphones, on the other hand, keep track of all the numbers you called. This information can be quite convenient, like when you want to return a call and you don't have that number handy. In addition, you can easily add a number to the contact list on your phone.

By tapping the Recent link on the phone screen, you get a list of all incoming and outgoing calls. (This hyperlink is located toward the top of the screen shown on the left side in Figure 3-2.) When you tap the Recent hyperlink, you see a call log like the one shown in Figure 3-6.

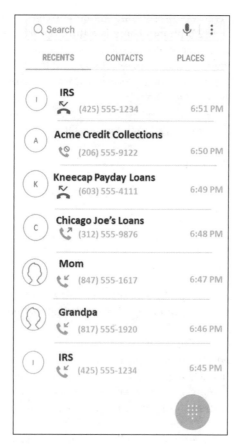

FIGURE 3-6:
A call log.

The tabs along the top include

» **Outgoing call you made:** An orange arrow points to the number.

» **Incoming call you received:** A green arrow points away from the number.

» **Incoming call you missed:** A red phone silhouette with a broken arrow.

» **Incoming call you ignored:** A blue slash sign is next to the phone number.

The log is a list of all the calls you made or were made to you. This is handy so that you can easily call someone again or call her back. By tapping any number in your call list, you see a screen like the one shown in Figure 3-7. From this screen, you can do several things:

» Call the number by tapping the green call button.

» Send a text to that number by tapping the orange envelope icon. (More on this in Chapter 4.)

» Make a video call if you're set up to do that.

» Tap the details icon to add the number to your contacts list. I cover contacts in more detail in Chapter 6.

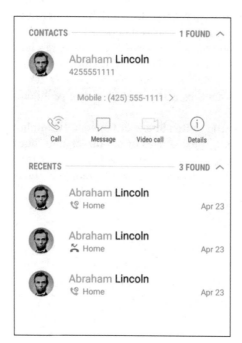

FIGURE 3-7:
Call Log detail.

CHAPTER 3 **Calling People** 55

Making an Emergency Call: The 411 on 911

Cellphones are wonderful tools for calling for help in an emergency. The Samsung Galaxy S8, like all phones in the United States and Canada, can make emergency calls to 911.

Just tap the Phone icon on the Home screen, tap 911, and then tap Send. You'll be routed to the 911 call center nearest to your location. This works wherever you're at within the United States. So, say you live in Chicago but have a car accident in Charlotte; just tap 911 to be connected to the 911 call center in Charlotte, not Chicago.

Even if your phone isn't registered on a network, you don't have a problem as long as you have a charge in the battery. You phone lets you know that the only number you can dial is a 911 call center, even if the Home screen is locked.

TIP

When you call 911 from a landline, the address you're calling from is usually displayed for the operator. When you're calling from a cellphone, though, the operator doesn't have that specific information. So, when you call 911, the operator might say, "911. *Where* is your emergency?" Don't let this question throw you; after all, you're probably focused on *what* is happening and not on *where*. Take a moment and come up with a good description of where you are — the street you're on, the nearest cross street (if you know it), any businesses or other landmarks nearby. An operator who knows where you are is in a better position to help you with your emergency. Your phone does have a GPS receiver in it that 911 centers can access. However, it's not always accurate; it may not be receiving location information at that moment, as is the case when you're indoors.

REMEMBER

When traveling outside the United States or Canada, 911 might not be the number you call in an emergency. Mexico uses 066, 060, or 080, but most tourist areas also accept 911. And most — but not all — of Europe uses 112. Knowing the local emergency number is as important as knowing enough of the language to say you need help.

WHEN YOU ACCIDENTALLY DIAL 911

If you accidentally dial 911 from your phone, don't hang up. Just tell the operator that it was an accidental call. She might ask some questions to verify that you are indeed safe and not being forced to say that your call was an accident.

If you panic and hang up after accidentally dialing 911, you'll get a call from the nearest 911 call center. Always answer the call, even if you feel foolish. If you don't answer the call, the 911 call centers will assume that you're in trouble and can't respond. They'll track you down from the GPS in your phone to verify that you're safe. If you thought you'd feel foolish explaining your mistake to a 911 operator, imagine how foolish you'd feel explaining it to the police officer who tracks you down and is upset with you for wasting the department's time.

Syncing a Bluetooth Headset

With a Bluetooth headset device, you can talk on your phone without having to hold the phone to your ear — and without any cords running from the phone to your earpiece. You've probably come across plenty of people talking on Bluetooth headsets. You might even have wondered whether they were a little crazy talking to themselves. Well, call yourself crazy now, because when you start using a Bluetooth headset, you might never want to go back.

Not surprisingly, Galaxy S8 phones can connect to Bluetooth devices. The first step to using a Bluetooth headset with your phone is to sync the two devices. Here's how:

1. **From the Home screen on your phone, slide up to get to the Apps screen.**

   This gets you to the list of all the applications on your phone.

2. **Flick or pan to the Settings icon and tap it.**

   The Settings icon is shown here. This screen holds most of the settings that you can adjust on your phone. If you prefer, you can also bring down the notification screen and tap the gear icon or tap the menu button on the Home screen. All these actions will get you to the same place.

   Tapping on the Settings icon brings up the screen shown in Figure 3-8.

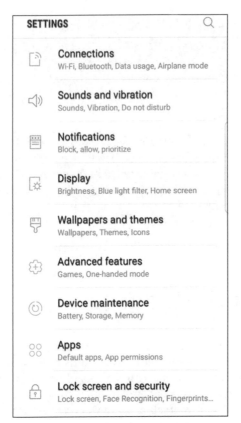

FIGURE 3-8:
The Settings
screen.

3. **Tap the Connections icon.**

   All the options for connectivity on your phone appear.

4. **Tap the Bluetooth icon.**

   This will bring up one of the two screens shown in Figure 3-9. If Bluetooth is off, it will looks like the screen to the left. If it is on, it will look like the screen on the right.

5. **Put the phone in to Pairing mode by turning on Bluetooth or by turning Bluetooth off and on again.**

   This step enables your phone to be visible to other Bluetooth devices. This state will last for about 60 seconds — enough time for you to get your Bluetooth device into pairing mode so that both devices can negotiate the proper security settings and pair up every time they "see" each other from now on. For example, the phone in the right image in Figure 3-9 recognizes its old friend, the Bose Color SoundLink. This device and the phone are shown in this image trying to re-establish a connection. The SoundLink and this phone had a connection at one time. That connection was broken. Now they want to pair up again. This is automatic once you exchange the correct security code.

Bluetooth in "Off" Mode

Bluetooth in "On" Mode

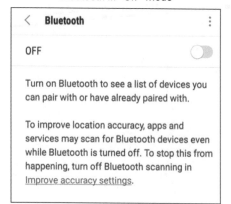

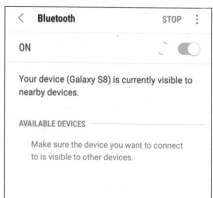

FIGURE 3-9:
The Bluetooth
Settings
screens.

6. **Next, put your headset into sync mode.**

   Follow the instructions that came with your headset.

   After a moment, the phone "sees" the headset. When it does, you're prompted to enter the security code, and the software keyboard pops up.

7. **Enter the security code for your headset and then tap the Enter button.**

TIP

   The security code on most headsets is 0000, but check the instructions that came with your headset if that number doesn't work.

   Your phone might see other devices in the immediate area. If so, it asks you which device you want to pair with. Tap the name of your headset.

   Your headset is now synced to your phone. If you turn one on when the other is already on, they recognize each other and automatically pair up.

Options Other than Headsets

Headsets are not the only option anymore. Although many people walk around with the ubiquitous Bluetooth headset dangling from an ear, many other choices are out there. You can sync to all kinds of Bluetooth devices, including external keyboards, laptops, tablets, external speakers, and even your car.

There are also external sensors for measuring blood pressure, heart rate, and a lot of other physical information. Some of these are built into wearable devices, like a fitness bracelet. Manufacturers are now embedding computers into home appliances that can also connect to your smartphone through Bluetooth!

The good news is that regardless of the technology, you can connect all these devices to your phone simply by using the steps described in the preceding section. I talk more about these possibilities in later chapters.

Chapter **4**

Discovering the Joy of Text

Sure, cellphones are made for talking. But these days, many people use their cellphones even more for texting.

Even the most basic phones support texting these days, but your Galaxy S8 phone makes sending and receiving text messages more convenient, no matter whether you're an occasional or pathological texter. In this chapter, I fill you in on how to send a text message (with or without an attachment), how to receive a text message, and how to read your old text messages.

TIP

This chapter uses images from the Samsung Messaging application. It is possible that your phone may have as its default another texting application. If so, you can easily switch to the Messaging app. You can also use the default app, but the images will be somewhat different. Your choice.

Sending the First Text Message

Text messages (which are short messages, usually 160 characters or less, sent by cellphone) are particularly convenient when you can't talk at the moment (maybe you're in a meeting or class) or when you just have a small bit of information to share ("Running late — see you soon!").

Many cellphone users — particularly younger ones — prefer sending texts to making a phone call. They find texting a faster and more convenient way to communicate, and they often use texting shorthand to fit more content in a short message.

There are two scenarios for texting. The first is when you send someone a text for the first time. The second is when you have a text conversation with a person.

When you first get your phone and are ready to brag about your new Galaxy S8 and want to send a text to your best friend, here's how easy it is:

1. **On the Home screen, tap the Messages icon.**

The Messages icon looks like an envelope. When you tap it, you will get a mostly blank Home screen for texting. This is shown in Figure 4-1.

When you have some conversations going, it begins to fill up.

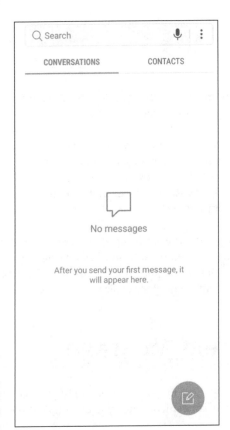

FIGURE 4-1: The initial Messaging Home screen.

2. **Tap the New Message icon (the pencil hovering over a blank page).**

   Tapping the New Message icon brings up the screen shown in Figure 4-2.

FIGURE 4-2:
A blank
texting screen.

3. **Tap to enter the recipient's ten-digit mobile telephone number.**

   A text box appears at the top of the screen with the familiar To field at the top. The keyboard appears at the bottom of the screen.

   As shown in Figure 4-3, the top field is where you type the telephone number. The numerals are along the top of the keyboard.

REMEMBER

   Be sure to include the area code, even if the person you're texting is local. There's no need to include a 1 before the number.

   If this is your first text, you haven't had a chance to build up a history of texts. After you've been using your messaging application for a while, you will have entered contact information, and your phone will start trying to anticipate your intended recipient. You can take one of its suggestions or you can just keep on typing.

Partially typed number with guesses

Fully typed number

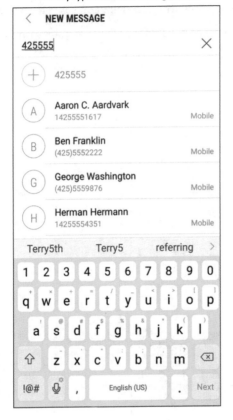

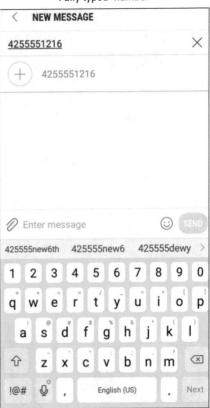

FIGURE 4-3:
Type the recipient's number in the upper text box.

4. **To type your text message, tap the text box that says Enter message. Figure 4-4 shows you where to enter your text.**

   Your message will appear in the text box to the right of the paper clip icon.

   In the Android Messaging app, your text message can be up to 160 characters, including spaces and punctuation. The application counts down the number of characters you have left.

   REMEMBER

5. **Send the text by tapping the Send button to the right of your message.**

   The Send button is grayed out before you start typing. After you type something, it turns full-on orange. Once you tap the button, the phone takes it from here. Within a few seconds, the message is sent to your friend's cellphone.

TIP

After you build your contact list (read about this in Chapter 6), you can tap a name from the contact list or start typing a name in the recipient text box. If there's only one number for that contact, your phone assumes that's the receiving phone you want to send a text to. If that contact has multiple numbers, it asks you which phone number you want to send your text to.

FIGURE 4-4:
Type your text.

REMEMBER

In most cases, the default for your texting app is for your phone to automatically correct what it thinks is a misspelled word. You can see it guess on the darker gray area under the text message. This capability is called *autocorrect.* You may find it very handy, or you may find it annoying. If you like it, you should still verify that it corrected the word in the right way. If you want evidence as to why this is a good idea, search "funny autocorrect examples" in your favorite search engine (although some can be very racy).

WARNING

You've probably heard a thousand times about how it's a very bad idea to text while you're driving. Here comes one-thousand-and-one. It's a *very bad idea* to text while you're driving — and illegal in some places. There are Dummies who read this book, who are actually very smart, and then there are DUMMIES who text and drive. I want you to be the former and not the latter.

Carrying on a Conversation via Texting

In the bad ol' pre-Galaxy S days, most cellular phones would keep a log of your texts. The phone kept the texts that you sent or received in sequential order, regardless of who sent or received them.

Texts stored sequentially are old-school. Your Galaxy S8 keeps track of the contact with whom you've been texting and stores each set of back-and-forth messages as a *conversation*.

In Figure 4-5, you can see that the first page for messaging holds *conversations*. After you start texting someone, those texts are stored in one conversation.

As Figure 4-5 shows, each text message is presented in sequence, with the author of the text indicated by the direction of the text balloon.

FIGURE 4-5: A messaging conversation.

Note the Enter message text box at the bottom of the screen. With this convenient feature, you can send whatever you type to the person with whom you're having a conversation.

In the bad old days, it was sometimes hard to keep straight the different texting conversations you were having. When you start a texting conversation with someone else, there is a second conversation.

Before too long, you'll have multiple conversations going on. Don't worry. They aren't the kind of conversations you need to keep going constantly. No one thinks twice if you don't text for a while. The image in Figure 4-6 shows how the text page from Figure 4-1 can look before too long.

TIP

It is easy to change the font size of conversations. To make the fonts larger and easier to read, use the stretch motion. Use the pinch motion to make the fonts smaller so that you can see more of the conversation.

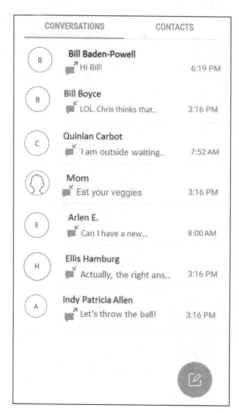

FIGURE 4-6:
The Text screen showing multiple conversations.

Sending an Attachment with a Text

What if you want to send something in addition to or instead of text? Say you want to send a picture, some music, or a Word document along with your text. Easy as pie, as long as the phone on the receiving end can recognize the attachment. Here is the recipe:

1. **From the Home screen, tap the Messages icon.**

2. **Either tap the New Message icon and enter the number of the intended recipient or pick up on an existing conversion.**

   You'll see the text creation page from Figure 4-2. Enter the information you want like a normal text.

3. **To add an attachment, tap the icon that looks like a paper clip to the left of where you enter text.**

   The paper-clip icon brings up the screen you see in Figure 4-7, which asks what kind of file you want to attach. Your choices include pictures, videos, audio files, and some others I describe in Chapters 9, 12, 13, and 14 when you have some good files to share. For now, it's just good that you know you have options.

FIGURE 4-7:
File types you
can attach
to a text.

4. **Tap your choice of file type, and your phone presents you with the options that fall into that category.**

   Get ready to be amazed. At the bottom of the screen, you have three choices. Figure 4-7 shows the Other category. This is for any file you want to attach that is already on your phone. It can be your electronic business card. It could be a video.

The middle option, Gallery, takes you to all the images you have stored on your phone. Samsung knows that the most common attachment is a photo. Tapping the Gallery options makes it that much easier.

The last option, going right to left, is the Camera. When you select this option, it opens up your camera so that you can take a picture and immediately send it to the recipient. How cool is that?!

5. **Continue typing your text message, if needed.**

6. **When you're done with the text portion of the message, tap the Send button, and off it all goes.**

TECHNICAL STUFF

A simple text message is an SMS (short message service) message. When you add an attachment, you're sending an MMS (multimedia messaging service) message. Back in the day, MMS messages cost more to send and receive than SMS messages did. These days, that isn't the case in the United States.

Receiving Text Messages

Receiving a text is even easier than sending one.

When you're having a text conversation and you get a new text from the person you're texting with, your phone beeps and/or vibrates. Also, the notification area of the screen (the very top) shows a very small version of the Messages icon.

You can either pull down the notification area from the very top of the screen or start the messaging application. Your choice.

If an attachment comes along, it's included in the conversation screen.

To access the text, you need to unlock the screen. The Messages icon (an envelope) also displays the number of new texts that you have. Tap that icon to open the conversations.

Managing Your Text History

The Messaging Conversations screen stores and organizes all your texts until you delete them. You should clean up this screen every now and then.

The simplest option for managing your messages is to tap the Menu icon and then tap Delete Threads. You can then select and unselect all the conversations that you want deleted. Tap the Delete link at the bottom of the screen, and they disappear.

Another deletion option is to open the conversation. You can delete each text by pressing and holding on the balloon. After a moment, a menu appears from which you can delete that message. This method is a lot slower if you have lots of texts, though.

I recommend that you be vicious in deleting the older texts and conversations. Trust me; deleting all your old messages can be cathartic!

Chapter **5**

Sending and Receiving Email

f you've had email on your phone for a while, you know how convenient it is. If your Galaxy S8 phone is your first cellphone with the capability to send and receive email, prepare to be hooked.

I start this chapter by showing you how to set up your email, regardless of whether your email program is supported. Then I show you how to read and manage your email. Finally, I tell you how to write and send email in the last section in this chapter.

Setting Up Your Email

These days, many people have multiple personal email address for many reasons. Your phone's Email app can manage up to ten email accounts. With a Galaxy S8 phone, you may need to create a separate email account on Google's Gmail just for your phone. If you do not get a Gmail account, you'll miss out on so many exciting capabilities. I highly recommend setting up a new Gmail account if you don't have one already (see the upcoming section "Setting up a new Gmail account).

The Email app on your phone routinely "polls" all the email systems for which you identify an email account and password. It then presents you with copies of your email.

TIP

Your phone mainly interacts with your inbox on your email account. It isn't really set up to work like the full-featured email application on your computer, though. For example, many email packages integrate with a sophisticated word processor, have sophisticated filing systems for your saved messages, and offer lots of fonts. As long as you don't mind working without these capabilities, you might never need to get on your computer to access your email again, and you could store email in folders on your phone.

Setup is easy, and having access to all your email makes you so productive that I advise you to consider adding all your email accounts to your phone.

Getting ready

In general, connecting to a personal email account simply involves entering the name of your email account(s) and its password(s) in your phone. Have these handy when you're ready to set up your phone.

As mentioned, you can have up to ten email accounts on your phone; however, you do need to pick one account as your favorite. You can send an email using any of the accounts, but your phone wants to know the email account that you want it to use as a default.

Next, you may want to have access to your work account. This is relatively common these days, but some companies see this as a security problem. You should consult with your IT department for some extra information. Technologically, it's not hard to make this kind of thing happen as long as your business email is reasonably modern.

Finally, if you don't already have a Gmail account, I strongly encourage you to get one. Read the nearby sidebar, "The advantages of getting a Gmail account" to find out why.

THE ADVANTAGES OF GETTING A GMAIL ACCOUNT

You might already have work and personal email accounts. You might even have an old email account that you check only once in a while because some friends, for whatever reason, haven't updated their profile for you and continue to use an old address.

The thought of getting yet another email address, even one that's free, might (understandably) be unappealing. After all, it's another address and password to remember. However, some important functions on your phone require a Gmail account:

- The ability to buy applications from the Google Play Store. (This is big!) I go over the Play Store in Chapter 8.

- The ability to use the Google Drive for storage. (This is pretty important and almost huge!)

- Free access to the photo site Google Photos (although other sites have many of the same features).

- Automatic backup of your contacts and calendar. That's explained in more detail in Chapters 6 and 13.

To make a long story short, it's worth the trouble to get a Gmail account, even if you already have a personal email account.

Setting up your existing Gmail account

If you already have a Gmail account, setting it up on your phone is easy as can be. Follow these steps from the Apps menu:

1. **Find the Gmail icon in the Apps list.**

   Here is a confusing part. The icon on the left in Figure 5-1 is the Gmail app. The icon on the right is for the general email app. The general email app is for your combined email accounts. The general email account is the app that you will use to access any and all of your email accounts.

2. **Tap the Gmail icon.**

   Because your phone does not know if you have a Gmail account yet, it offers you the option of entering your Gmail account or whether you want to create a new account. This page is shown in Figure 5-2.

FIGURE 5-1:
The Email and Gmail icons.

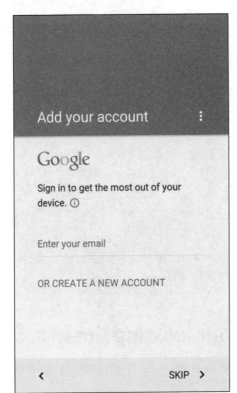

FIGURE 5-2:
Add your account page.

3. **Enter your Gmail account email address and tap Next.**

   Be sure to include the @gmail.com suffix. Tapping Next brings up the screen shown in Figure 5-3.

4. **Enter your existing Gmail password and tap Next.**

   Go ahead and type your password. When you're ready, tap Next on the keyboard.

You may get a pop-up reconfirming that you agree with the terms of use and all that legal stuff. Tap OK. You'll see lots of flashing lights and whirling circles while your phone and your Gmail account get to know each other.

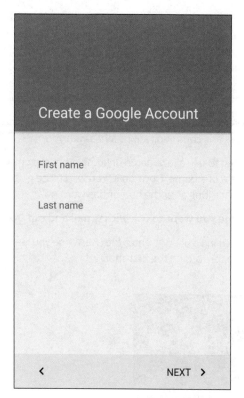

FIGURE 5-3:
Enter your first
and last name
on this screen.

If everything is correct, your phone and your account get acquainted and become best friends. After a few minutes, they are ready to serve your needs. There are even a few screens that tell you all the wonderful things that your Gmail account will do for you. Believe every word!

If you have a problem, you probably mistyped something. Try retyping your information. From this point on, any email you get in your Gmail account will also appear on your phone!

Setting up a new Gmail account

If you need to set up a new Gmail account, you have a few more steps to follow. Before you get into the steps, think up a good user ID and password.

TIP

Gmail has been around for a while. That means all the good, simple email addresses are taken. Unless you plan to start using this email account as your main email, which you could do if you wanted, you're probably best off if you pick some unusual combination of letters and numbers that you can remember for now to get through this process.

When you have all of this ready, follow Steps 1 and 2 in the previous section, but tap the Or Create a New Account link when you get to the screen shown in Figure 5-2. From there, follow these steps:

1. **Enter your first and last names on the screen and tap Next.**

   Google asks for your name in the screen shown in Figure 5-3. This is how Google personalizes any communications it has with you.

TIP

   You may be tempted to use a fake name or some other clever two-word combination in place of a name. Don't do it. You will still be getting email to Rita Book or Warren Peace long after the humor has worn off.

2. **Enter the username you want to use with Gmail and tap Done.**

   On the screen shown in Figure 5-4, enter the username you want. Hopefully you get this name approved on the first shot.

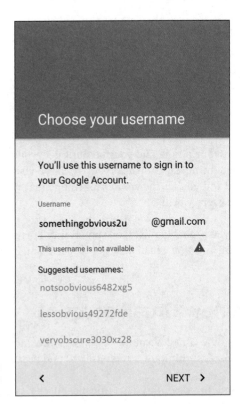

FIGURE 5-4:
The Username
screen.

If your first choice isn't available, try again. There is no easy way to check before you go through these steps. Eventually, you hit on an unused ID, or you will use one of the suggestions in blue font. When you're successful, it will congratulate you.

3. **Accept the terms and conditions of the account.**

   You may want a lawyer to review these terms and conditions. Or not. Basically, the terms are that you should be nice and not try to cheat anyone. Don't abuse the privilege of having the account.

4. **Prepare a security question and an alternate email address and tap Done or Skip.**

   If you forget your password, Google wants to verify that you're really you and not someone pretending to be you. Google does this check by sending a confirmation email to another account or sending a text to your phone. You can do this now or tap Skip to do it later.

After you tap Done, light flashes, and you see the screen working away. This process usually takes less than two minutes. While you wait, you'll see all kinds of messages that it's getting ready to sync things. Don't worry. I explain these messages in good time. For now, you can add any other email accounts you want by following the steps in the next section.

Working with non-Gmail email accounts

Your phone is set up to work with up to ten email accounts. If you have more than ten accounts, I'm thinking that you might have too much going on in your life. No phone, not even the Galaxy S8, can help you there!

I now cover the steps to adding your email accounts. Once you tell your phone all your email accounts, the Email screen will let you see the inbox of each account or combine all your email in a single inbox. You can choose which option works best for you.

Adding your first email account

To get started, have your email addresses and passwords ready. When you have them, go to your phone's Home screen. Look for the Mail icon; it is an envelope with an @ on it (refer to Figure 5-1). This is probably on your Home screen as one of the four primary shortcuts just above the Device Function keys or in your application list.

1. **Tap the Menu icon from the Email screen.**

   This brings up a menu like the one shown in Figure 5-5 with the options to set up an email account. It is then simply a matter of entering your email address and password. Otherwise, continue on.

FIGURE 5-5:
The menu for the Email app.

2. **Tap the Add Others Account icon.**

    This is a generic way to enter lots of kinds of email accounts. Email accounts on Yahoo!, AOL, Outlook.com, or another email service work from the screen shown in Figure 5-6.

3. **Carefully enter your full email account name and then enter your password in the second field.**

WARNING

    Your email address should include the full shebang, including the @ sign and everything that follows it. Make sure to enter your password correctly, being careful with capitalization if your email server is case-sensitive (most are). If in doubt, select the option that lets you see your password.

4. **Tap Next.**

    You see all kinds of options you can select. Just go with the default settings for now. This brings up the screen shown in Figure 5-7.

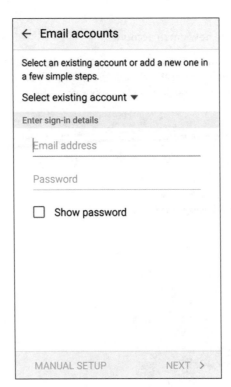

FIGURE 5-6:
The Add Account screen.

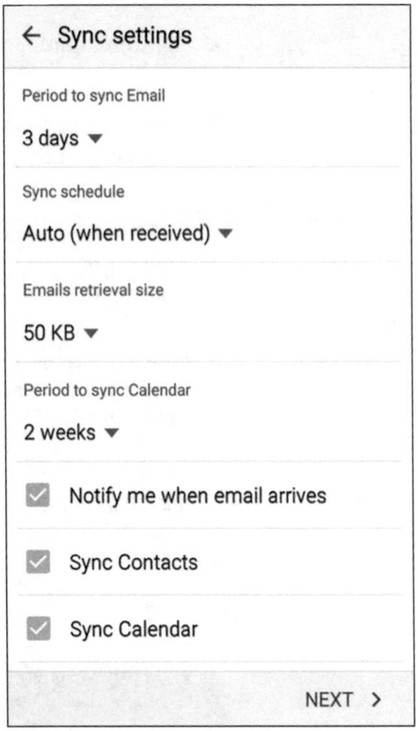

FIGURE 5-7:
The Sync Settings screen.

5. **Select your desired Sync Settings and then tap Next.**

You can select how often you want your phone and the email service to synchronize. A lot of thought and consideration has been put into the default settings. If you just want to get started, tap Next.

If you want to fine-tune things later, it is not hard to go back and adjust these settings. These settings are intended to be gentle on your data usage.

If you want images in email to download immediately, store older email messages on your phone, check to see whether you have new email all the time, you can change these settings on this page for this email account. If you know what you want that is different from the default settings, make the changes and then tap Next.

6. Enter a name for the new email account.

The next screen is shown in Figure 5-8. This gives you the option to call your email account something other than its address. You can always use the email address for the name, but I recommend choosing something shorter, like Joe's MSN or My Hotmail.

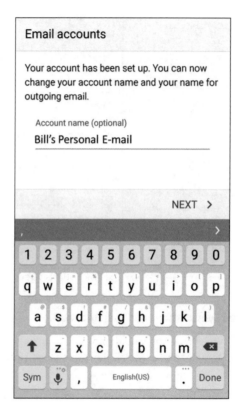

FIGURE 5-8: Naming your email account.

7. Tap Done.

Using Figure 5-9 as an example, you can see that my account is now registered on my phone. It worked!

Options icon

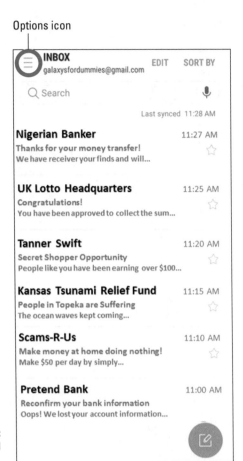

INBOX
galaxysfordummies@gmail.com

EDIT   SORT BY

Q Search

Last synced 11:28 AM

Nigerian Banker   11:27 AM
Thanks for your money transfer!
We have receiver your finds and will...

UK Lotto Headquarters   11:25 AM
Congratulations!
You have been approved to collect the sum...

Tanner Swift   11:20 AM
Secret Shopper Opportunity
People like you have been earning over $100...

Kansas Tsunami Relief Fund   11:15 AM
People in Topeka are Suffering
The ocean waves kept coming...

Scams-R-Us   11:10 AM
Make money at home doing nothing!
Make $50 per day by simply...

Pretend Bank   11:00 AM
Reconfirm your bank information
Oops! We lost your account information...

FIGURE 5-9:
The Email
Home screen.

Adding additional email accounts

Once you have entered your first email account, there are a few different steps to add additional accounts.

1. **Tap the Options icon at the top-left part of the screen.**

   The three horizontal lines bring up the slide-in screen shown in Figure 5-10. This allows you to see other email folders. It also lets you access the setting icon.

2. **Tap the Settings icon.**

   Tapping Settings brings up the screen shown in Figure 5-11.

3. **Tap Add Account next to the green plus sign.**

   This brings you back to the Set up email screen (refer to Figure 5-5).

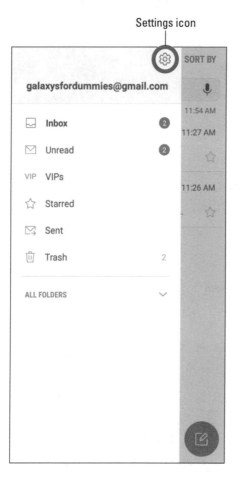

Settings icon

galaxysfordummies@gmail.com

SORT BY

11:54 AM

☐ Inbox ②

11:27 AM

✉ Unread ②

VIP VIPs

11:26 AM

☆ Starred

✉ Sent

🗑 Trash 2

ALL FOLDERS ⌄

FIGURE 5-10:
The Options
slide-in screen.

At this point you can add up to nine more accounts, and remember, you will be asked which email account you want to be your primary account. It is entirely up to you. You can send and receive email from all your accounts by selecting it, but only one can be the primary account used if you send an email from another application, such as the Contacts app.

Setting up a corporate email account

In addition to personal email accounts, you can add your work email account to your phone — if it's based upon a Microsoft Exchange server, that is, and if it's okay with your company's IT department.

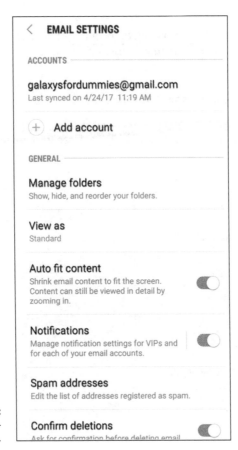

FIGURE 5-11:
The Email Set-
tings screen.

Before you get started, you need some information from the IT department of your company:

» The domain name of the office email server

» Your work email password

» The name of your exchange server

If the folks in IT are okay with you using your phone to access its email service, your IT department will have no trouble supplying you with this information.

WARNING

Before you set up your work email on your phone, make sure that you have permission. If you do this without the green light from your company, and you end up violating your company's rules, you could be in hot water. Increasing your productivity won't be much help if you're standing out in the parking lot holding all the contents of your office in a cardboard box.

Assuming that your company wants you to be more productive with no extra cost to the company, the process for adding your work email starts at your email Home screen shown in Figure 5-5.

1. **Enter your email address and password.**

The Corporate screen is shown in Figure 5-12. It is similar to the screen shown in Figure 5-6, but this time, in Figure 5-12, I have closed the keypad and you can see the full screen.

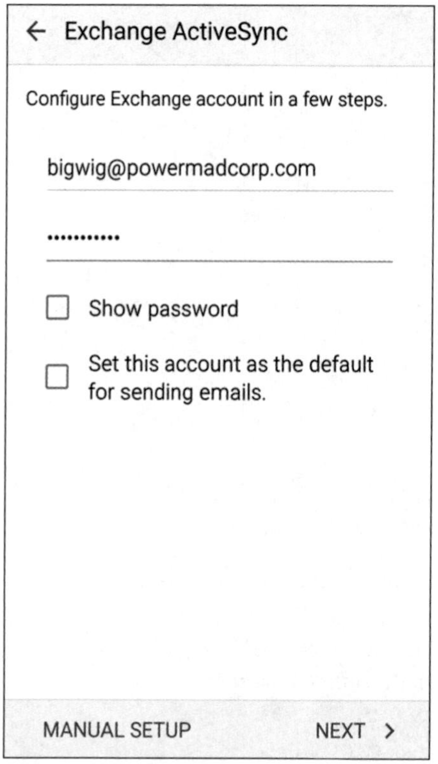

FIGURE 5-12: The Corporate set up email screen.

2. **Tap Manual Setup.**

This brings up the screen shown in Figure 5-13.

The chances are that you haven't got the foggiest notion what any of this means or what you are to do now.

3. **Verify that your IT department is good with you having email on your own device and have them give you the necessary settings.**

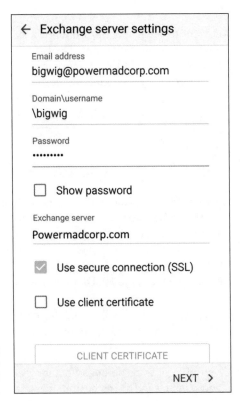

FIGURE 5-13:
The Manual
Setup screen
for adding
corporate
email
accounts.

Seriously. It is increasingly common that a firm will give you access on your phone. At the same time, they do not generally circulate documents with how to make this happen. This would be a big security problem if anyone could get access. Save yourself the time and get help from IT.

Reading Email on Your Phone

In Figure 5-9, you can see how the email screen looks for what I have called My Personal Email. You can also set it up so that this screen is set up so that it combines all your email into one inbox. At any given time, you might want to look at the accounts individually or all together.

To look at all your email in one large inbox, tap the downward pointing arrow next to the word Inbox and select Combined Inbox. This lists all your email in chronological order. To open any email message, just tap it.

If, on the other hand, you want to see just email from one account, tap the box at the top that says Combined Inbox. When you tap this icon, your phone will display all the individual email accounts. Tap on the account you want to focus on at the moment, and your phone will bring up your email in chronological order for just that email address.

Writing and Sending Email

After you set up the receiving part of email, the other important side is composing and sending email. At any time when you're in an email screen, simply tap the Menu button to get a pop-up screen. From the pop-up menu, tap the Compose icon to open the email composition screen.

Here's the logic that determines which email account will send this email:

>> If you're in the inbox of an email account and you tap the Compose icon after tapping Menu, your phone sends the email to the intended recipient(s) through that account.

>> If you're in the combined inbox or some other part of the email app, your phone assumes that you want to send the email from the default email account that you selected when you registered your second (or additional) email account.

When you tap the Compose icon in the Menu pop-up menu, it tells you which account it will use. The Email composition screen shown in Figure 5-14 says this email will be coming from this account: galaxysfordummies@gmail.com.

As shown in this screen, the top has a stalwart To field, where you type the recipient's address. You can also call up your contacts, a group, or your most recent email addresses. (Read all about contacts in Chapter 6.) Tap the address or contact you want, and it populates the To field.

Below that, in the Subject field, is where you enter the email's topic. And below that is the body of the message, with the default signature, Sent from my Samsung Galaxy S8, although your cellular carrier might have customized this signature.

FIGURE 5-14:
The Email
composition
screen.

At the top of the screen are three links:

>> **Attach:** Tap this hyperlink to attach a file of any variety to your email.

>> **Send:** Tap this link to send the email to the intended recipient(s).

>> **More (three vertical dots):** Tap this option, and you get the pop-up shown in Figure 5-15. This gives you the following options:

- **Save in Drafts:** This allows you to complete the email later without losing your work.

- **Send email to myself:** This is an alternative to saving the email in your Sent mail folder.

- **Priority:** This option signifies that this is more important that the average email to your recipients.

- **Security options:** You have some fancy, 007 options here. You can sign the document or encrypt it.

- **Turn on Rich text:** To save data usage, email is sent in a default font. If you want to burn at little more data, you can get creative and add more elaborate fonts.

Save in Drafts

Send email to myself

Priority

Security options

Turn on Rich text

FIGURE 5-15:
Composition
email options.

If you change your mind about sending an email message, you can just tap the Back key. If you're partially done with the message, you're asked whether you want to save it in your Drafts folder.

The Drafts folder works like the Drafts folder in your computer's email program. When you want to continue working on a saved email, you open the Drafts folder, tap on it, and continue working.

Replying To and Forwarding Email

Replying to or forwarding the email that you get is a common activity. You can do this from your Email app. Figure 5-16 shows a typical open email message.

You can reply by tapping the icon with the return arrow at the bottom of the screen. If other people were copied on the email, you could tap the double return arrow to Reply all.

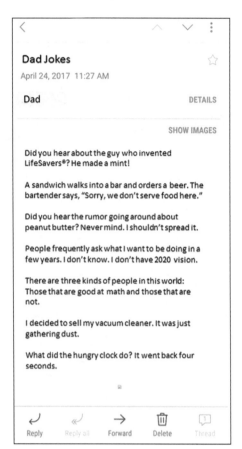

FIGURE 5-16: An opened email.

When you tap either of these options, the Reply screen comes back with the To line populated by the sender's email address (or addresses) and a blank space where you can leave your comments. (In the case of Figure 5-16, you could ask that your dad not send you any more jokes like these.)

To forward the email, tap the arrow pointing to the right above the word Forward and enter the addressee just as you do when sending a new email.

Chapter **6**

Managing Your Contacts

You're probably familiar with using contact databases. Many cellphones automatically create one, or at least prompt you to create one. You also probably have a file of contacts on your work computer, made up of work email addresses and telephone numbers. And if you have a personal email account, you probably have a contact database of email accounts of friends and family members. If you're kickin' it old school, you might even keep a paper address book with names, addresses, and telephone numbers.

The problem with having all these contact databases is that it's rarely ever as neat and tidy as I've just outlined. A friend might email you at work, so you have her in both your contact databases. Then her email address might change, and you update that information in your personal address book but not in your work one. Before long, you have duplicate and out-of-date contacts, and it's hard to tell which is correct. How you include Facebook or LinkedIn messaging in your contact profile is unclear.

In addition to problems keeping all your contact databases current, it can be a hassle to migrate the database from your old phone. Some cellular carriers or firms have offered a service that converts your existing files to your new phone, but it's rarely a truly satisfying experience. You end up spending a lot of time correcting the assumptions it makes.

You now face that dilemma again with your Galaxy S8: deciding how to manage your contacts. This chapter gives you the advantages of each approach so that you can decide which one will work best for you. That way, you won't have the frustration of wishing you had done it another way before you put 500 of your best friends in the wrong filing system.

Using the Galaxy S8 Contacts App

Your phone wants you to be able to communicate with all the people you would ever want to in any way you know how to talk to them. This is a tall order, and your Galaxy S8 makes it as easy as possible. In fact, I wouldn't be surprised if the technology implemented in the Contacts app becomes one of your favorite capabilities of the phone. After all, your phone is there to simplify communication with friends, family, and coworkers, and the Contacts app on your phone makes it as easy as technology allows.

At the same time, this information is only as good as your contact database discipline. The focus of this section is to help you help your phone help you.

Learning the Contacts App on your phone

The fact of the matter is, if you introduced your phone to your email accounts in Chapter 5, the Contacts list on your phone has all the contacts from each of your contact lists.

Take a look at it and see. From your Home screen, tap the Contacts icon.

If you haven't created a Gmail account, synced your personal email, or created a contact when you sent a text or made a call, your Contacts list will be empty. Otherwise, you see a bunch of your contacts now residing on your phone, sorted alphabetically (as shown in Figure 6-1).

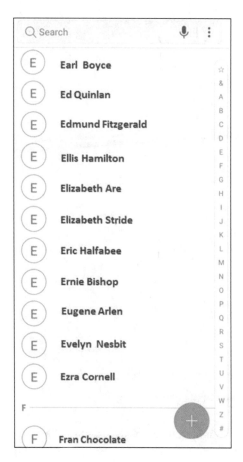

FIGURE 6-1:
The Contacts
list.

Along with the Contacts application that manages the data, this database does more than just store names, phone numbers, and email addresses. However, you can have the contact include any or all of the following information:

» All telephone numbers, including

- Mobile
- Home
- Work
- Work fax
- Pager
- Other

- » Email addresses
  - Home
  - Work
  - Mobile
- » Instant Messaging addresses
- » Company/organization
- » Job title
- » Nickname
- » Mailing address for
  - Home
  - Work
  - Another location
- » Any notes about this person
  - Web address
  - Birthday (or other significant event)
  - A phonetic spelling of the name

As if all this weren't enough, you can assign a specific ringtone to play when a particular person contacts you. I cover the steps to assign a music file to an individual caller in Chapter 12.

Finally, you can assign a picture for the contact. It can be one out of your Gallery; you can take a new picture; or (as I discuss in Chapter 8) you can connect to a social network like Facebook and use that person's profile picture.

Fortunately, the only essential information is a name. Every other field is optional and is only displayed if the field contains information to be displayed. Figure 6-2 shows a lightly populated contact.

FIGURE 6-2:
A lightly
populated
contact.

Deciding where to store your contacts

Before we get too far, it is important for you to decide the default option where you want to store your contacts. Deciding this now with the information this section provides you will make your life much easier as you go forward. It is possible to combine contact databases, but even the best tools are imperfect.

The first time you try to save a new contact, the Contacts App will offer you a pop-up screen, as shown in Figure 6-3. This lists the options you have and will take your first entry as the option you want as a default.

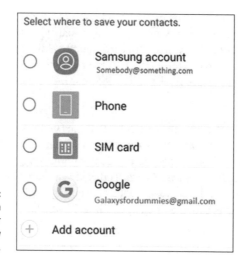

FIGURE 6-3:
Choosing a
default for
creating new
contacts.

Whenever you save a new entry, you can manually switch to another of these databases. Save yourself some time and aggravation and decide now what you want to do. Here are your options on where to save new contacts:

>> Within the memory of your phone

>> On the SIM card inserted in your phone

>> Within your Gmail account

>> As a contact in one of your other accounts

Each of these four options has advantages and disadvantages. If you simply want my advice, I suggest using your Gmail account to store new contacts. If this satisfies you, skip to the next section on linking contacts from other sources. Read on if you need some context.

Here is the deal: If everything is working properly, all options work equally well. However, if you switch phones regularly, ever lose you phone, need to make significant updates to your contacts, or are frequently out of wireless coverage, such as on an airplane, you should consider the options.

The first option mentioned involves storing your contacts within your phone. This is a great option, as long as you have your phone. However, there will come a day when Samsung (or HTC, or LG, and so on) has something faster and better, and you will want to upgrade. At that point, perhaps next year or in ten years, you will need to move your contacts to another location if you want to keep them. Plus, if you lose your phone, I sure hope that you have recently used one of the backup options I explore in Chapter 17.

The second option is to store your new contacts on your SIM card. The SIM card is familiar technology if your previous phone worked with AT&T or T-Mobile. Figure 6-4 shows a profile of a typical SIM card, next to a dime for scale, although yours probably has the logo of your cellular carrier nicely printed on the card. To the right of the SIM card is the newer micro SIM card. This is the same idea, but in a smaller package.

TECHNICAL STUFF

If your cellular carrier is Verizon, Sprint, or US Cellular, you may be confused. Your Galaxy S8 has a SIM card. What's the story? These carriers use CDMA technology for voice and for some data features. Up to 3G, the phones using CDMA technology and data services didn't use a SIM card. Today, *all* carriers in the United States are implementing a super high-speed data technology called LTE, also called 4G. Because your phone is capable of LTE, you now have a SIM card.

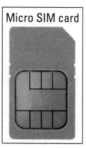

FIGURE 6-4:
A SIM card
and a micro
SIM card.

The cool aspect of using your SIM card is that you can pluck it out of your existing phone and pop it in another phone and all your contacts come with you. It works this easily if you stay with an Android smartphone of recent vintage. It almost works this easily if you, say, switch back to a feature phone (as in the kind of phone that merely makes calls and texts and costs $1). Another advantage is that your SIM card does not rely on having a wireless connection to update changes.

The next option is to store new contacts on your Gmail account. What this means is that your new contacts are automatically copied from your phone to the Gmail account of Google servers. This keeps the records on your phone, but Google maintains a copy of this record in your Gmail account. You can make changes to a contact on your phone or on your PC.

The two reasons I recommend using your Gmail account are

>> You can maintain these records with your full-sized keyboard rather than the smaller keyboard on your phone.

>> It is easy to get back all these contacts on a new Android phone simply by telling the new phone your Gmail account. Because you will probably enter your Gmail account right away when you get a new phone, your contacts reappear quicker than the fourth option.

The fourth option is to store the contacts in one of your existing email accounts. This may be the best option if you already consider your email, either your personal or work account, to be the primary location where you store contacts. If you already have good database discipline with one of your email accounts, by all means, use this email account as the default place to store new contacts.

If this particular account you currently use for keeping your contacts is not set up yet on your phone, you can tap the Add New Account link shown in Figure 6-3 to go through the process described in Chapter 5 to set up a new email account.

Linking Contacts on your phone

The Contacts list is smart. Allow me to explain some of the things that are going on.

Say your best friend is Bill McCarty, affectionately known as "the Kid." You sent Bill a text earlier to let him know about your new phone. You followed the instructions on how to send a text in Chapter 4 and entered his telephone number. You took it to the next step and tapped Add Contact. When you were prompted to add his name, you did. Now your phone has a contact, "Bill McCarty."

Then you linked your email. Of course your buddy Bill is in your email Contacts list. So while you were reading this chapter, several things happened. First, your phone and your Gmail account synced. Your phone thinks about it and figures this must be the same person. It automatically combines all the information in one entry on your phone!

Then your phone automatically updates your Gmail account. On the left side of Figure 6-5, you see the Google logo just beneath Bill's mobile number. This contact is synced with your Gmail account. You didn't have to do anything to make this happen.

FIGURE 6-5:
Two contacts
for the same
person.

Link Icons

Your phone noticed that Bill's work number was in your email contact information, but the mobile phone number you used to text him was not. No problem! Now the contact on your phone includes both the information you had in your email contact as well as his cellular phone.

Now, as slick as this system is, it isn't perfect. In this scenario, both contacts have the same first and last name. However, if the same person also goes by a different name, you have to link these contacts. For example, if you created a contact for Bill McCarty, but your email refers to him as William H. McCarty, your phone will assume that these are two different people.

No problem, though. Do you see the chain links icon in Figure 6-5 in the box that says Connected via? Here are the steps to link the two contacts for the same person:

1. **From a contact, tap on the chain icon.**

   This brings up the pop-up shown in Figure 6-6.

TIP

   Choose the contact whose name you want to be the primary name. For example, I tapped the link on the Bill McCarty contact, which is saved in Gmail. This will be the name used on the combined contact going forward.

FIGURE 6-6: The Linking Page for Bill McCarty.

2. **Tap the Link Another Contact link at the bottom of the screen.**

   Your phone will try to help you with some suggestions. If it gets it all wrong, you can just find the other contact by searching alphabetically, as shown in Figure 6-7.

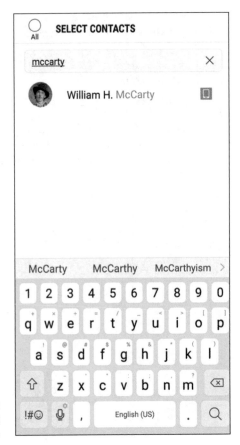

FIGURE 6-7: Some linking suggestions.

3. **Tap the contact you want joined.**

   In this case, the second guess, William H. McCarty, is the one you want. Tap the selection box to the left of his name. The result is shown in Figure 6-8.

4. **Now tap the link that says Link in the upper-right corner of the screen.**

   This combined link will now have all the information on this one person.

Let no man put this link asunder (unless you made a mistake and want to change it. Then go tap the chain icon to break the link).

TIP

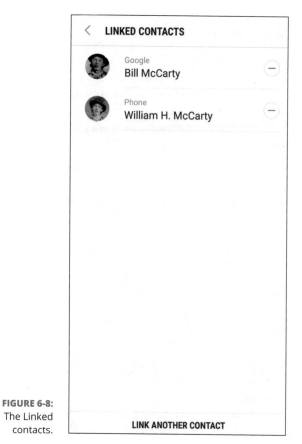

FIGURE 6-8:
The Linked
contacts.

Creating Contacts within Your Database

Your phone is out there trying to make itself the ultimate contact database with as little effort on your part as possible. The interesting thing is that the salesperson in the cellular store probably didn't explain this to you in detail. It's a subtle-but-important capability that's hard to communicate on the sales floor. Here's what happens.

Whenever you make or receive a call, send or receive an email, or send or receive a text, your phone looks up the telephone number or email address from which the message originated to check whether it has seen that address before. If it has, it has all the other information on that person ready. If it doesn't recognize the originating telephone number or email, it asks whether you want to make it a new contact or update an existing one. What could be easier?

Adding contacts as you dial

When you get a call, a text, or an email from someone who isn't in your contacts, you're given the option to create a profile for that person. The same is true when you initiate contact with someone who isn't in your Contacts list. Chapter 3 shows you the empty and full dialing screens. The image on the left in Figure 6-9 shows the phone trying its best to anticipate the person you are in the process of calling, and, if it is not saved already, the image on the right shows how it offers you the option to add this number to your contacts.

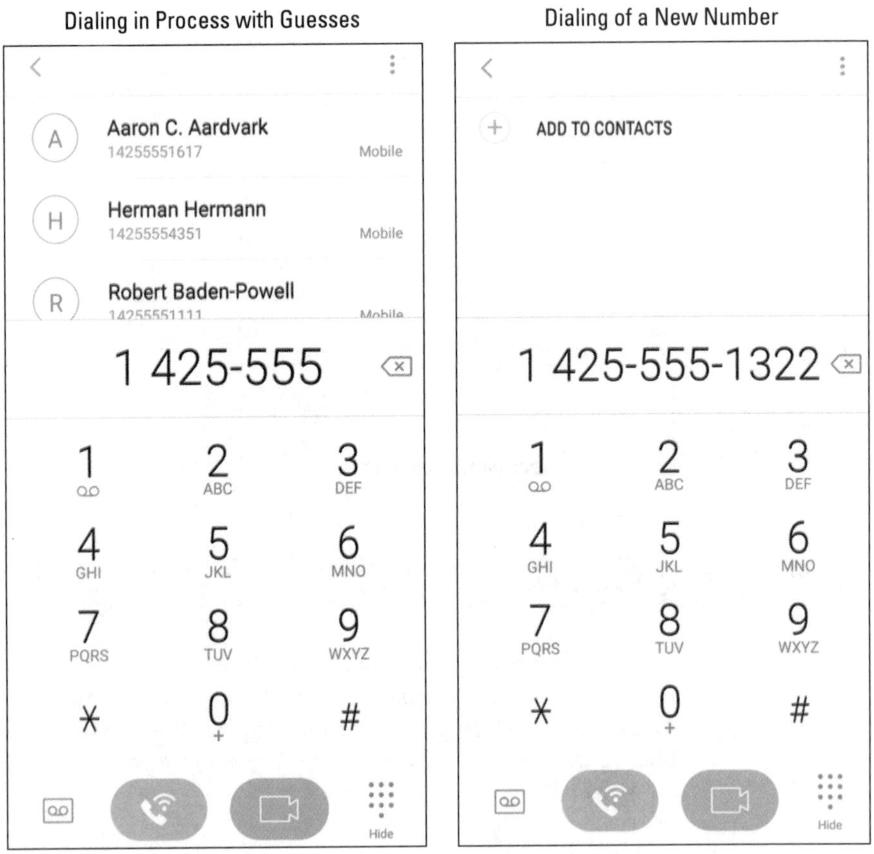

Dialing in Process with Guesses

Dialing of a New Number

FIGURE 6-9:
The dialing screens in process and when there is a new number.

When you tap Add to Contacts, you're immediately given the option to create a contact or update an existing contact. Your phone doesn't know whether this is a new number for an existing contact or a totally new person. Rather than make an assumption (as lesser phones on the market would do), your phone asks you whether you need to create a new profile or add this contact information to an existing profile.

TIP

Keep in mind that if you are calling an existing contact and your phone guesses the right person, you can save yourself time and tap the phone to dial.

Say that you want to enter this number as a new contact. You follow these steps:

1. **Tap the Add a Contact link.**

   It will first check to see whether you want to create a new contact or add this number to an existing contact. The Add to Contacts pop-up as shown in Figure 6-10 gives you these options. If this is a new number for an existing contact, this pop-up saves you from having to link contacts.

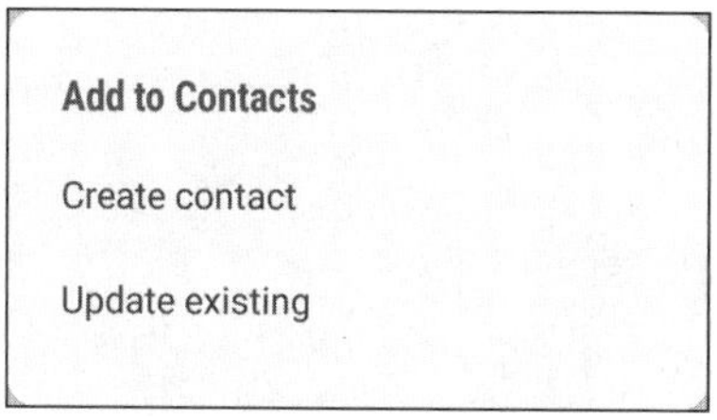

Add to Contacts

Create contact

Update existing

FIGURE 6-10:
The Add to
Contacts
pop-up.

2. **Tap the Create Contact link.**

   Tapping this link brings up a new contact page. An example is shown in Figure 6-11.

   The number is already populated. You just need to fill in the correct name plus any other information that you want associated with this person.

3. **When you're done typing in the information for this contact, tap Save at the top of the contact.**

   Figure 6-11 shows the Save button at the top of the screen.

Adding contacts manually

Adding contacts manually involves taking an existing contact database and adding its entries to your phone, one profile at a time. (This option, a last resort, was the only option for phones back in the day.)

1. **Tap the Contacts icon.**

   Doing so brings up the list of existing contacts shown in Figure 6-1.

The Save option

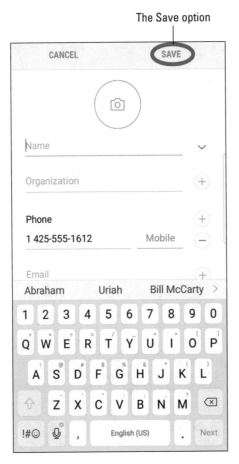

FIGURE 6-11:
A partially
populated
contact.

2. Tap the Add Contacts icon (the + [plus] sign next to a silhouette).

This icon is shown in Figure 6-12. Tapping it will bring up a blank contact page with nothing populated.

FIGURE 6-12:
The Add
Contacts icon.

3. **Fill in the information you want to include.**

4. **When you're done entering data, tap Save at the top of the screen.**

   The profile is now saved. Repeat the process for as many profiles as you want to create.

How Contacts Make Life Easy

Phew. Heavy lifting over. After you populate the profiles of dozens or hundreds of contacts, you're rewarded with a great deal of convenience.

Start by tapping a contact. You see that person's profile, as shown in Figure 6-13.

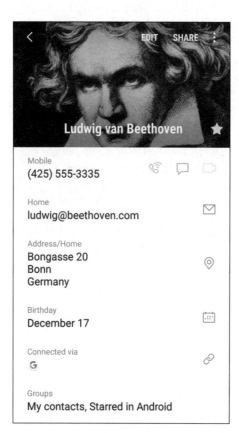

FIGURE 6-13: A typical profile.

All the options you have for contacting this contact are but a simple tap away:

» Tap the green telephone next to the number to dial that number.

» Tap the amber message icon to send a text.

» Tap the email icon to create an email.

About the only thing that tapping on a data field won't do is print an envelope for you if you tap the mailing address!

Playing Favorites

Over the course of time, you'll probably find yourself calling some people more than others. It would be nice to not have to scroll through your entire contacts database to find those certain people. Contacts allow you to place some of your contacts into a Favorites list for easy access.

From within the Contacts app, open the profile and notice the star next to that person's name (refer to Figure 6-13). To the right of the contact name is a star. If that star is gold, that contact is a Favorite. If not, then not.

To make a contact into a star, tap the blank outline of the star. To demote a contact from stardom without deleting, tap the gold star.

You won't immediately see a difference in your contacts other than the appearance of the gold star. When you open your phone, however, this contact now appears under your Favorites tab. The Favorites tab is like a mini-contact database. It looks similar in structure to your regular contact database, but it includes only your favorites.

3
Living on the Internet

Chapter **7**

You've Got the Whole (Web) World in Your Hands

If you're like most people, one of the reasons you got a smartphone is because you want Internet access on the go. You don't want to have to wait until you get back to your laptop or desktop to find the information you need online. You want to be able to access the Internet even when you're away from a Wi-Fi hotspot — and that's exactly what you can do with your Galaxy S8 phone. In this chapter, I show you how.

The browser that comes standard with your Galaxy S8 works almost identically to the browser that's currently on your PC. You see many familiar toolbars, including the Favorites bar and search engine. And the mobile version of the browser includes tabs that allow you to open multiple Internet sessions simultaneously.

This chapter goes into much more detail on using the Internet browser on your Galaxy S8, as well as the websites you can access from your phone, and discusses some of the trade-offs you can make when viewing a web page.

Starting the Browser

You have three options for getting access to information from the Internet via your Galaxy S8 phone. Which one you use is a personal choice. The choices are

» **Use the regular web page:** This option involves accessing a web page via its regular address (URL) and having the page come up on your screen. The resulting text may be small.

» **Use the mobile web page:** Many websites offer a mobile version of their regular web page. This is an abbreviated version of the full website that can be more easily read on a mobile device.

» **Find out whether a mobile app is associated with the web page:** Many websites have found that it is most expedient to write a mobile application to access the information on its website. The app reformats the web page to fit better on a mobile screen — a convenient option if you plan to access this website regularly. I cover the trade-offs about this option later in the section "Deciding Between Mobile Browsing and Mobile Apps" and explore how to find and install such apps in Chapter 8.

With this background, head to the Internet. On your Galaxy S8 phone, you may have a few choices on how to get there. Figure 7-1 shows three possible icons that can get you there. Tap any of these, and you can start surfing.

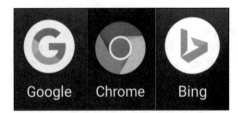

FIGURE 7-1:
Possible paths to the Internet on your Galaxy S8.

If you want a little more understanding as to why there are multiple options, read the nearby sidebar on Internet terminology.

For your purpose, tap either the Chrome icon or the Google icon to get started. These icons will typically be on the Home screen. Alternatively, tap the Application icon and find the Chrome or Google icon.

TIP

If you love Bing, you are not out of luck. Bing is either on your phone, or you can get it installed (I cover how to install things like Bing in Chapter 8). For now, just stay with Chrome and Google. Things on other browsers and search engines are mostly similar, and choosing the Chrome/Google pair simplifies things.

BASIC INTERNET TERMINOLOGY FOR DUMMIES

The term *Internet access* can mean a few different things. In some circumstances, the word Internet can mean a web browser. A *web browser* is an app that will display pages on the Internet. In other circumstances, the word Internet may refer to a search engine. You use a *search engine* to find either information you are seeking or to bring you to a website. Then you use a web browser to look at the information. Chances are the web browser on your phone that you will use is an app from Google called Chrome.

The chances are that the search engine you use on your phone is Google, but it may be the search engine for Microsoft called Bing. The goal with your phone is to get you where you want with minimal fuss. It is easier for the people that are bringing you this phone and service (Samsung, Google, and your wireless carrier) to give you three icons that essentially point to the same thing than to explain the terminology. Tapping the Internet icon, the Chrome icon, or the Google icon will most likely bring up the Chrome web browser.

As long as you're connected to the Internet (that is, you are either near a Wi-Fi hotspot or in an area where you have cellular service), your home page appears. If you tap the Google icon, it will be Google. If you tap Chrome, your default home page could be blank or the Google home page, but many cellular carriers set their phones' home pages to their own websites.

If you're out of coverage range or you turned off the cellular and Wi-Fi radios because you turned on Airplane mode, you get a pop-up screen letting you know that there is no Internet connection. (Read about Airplane mode in Chapter 2.)

TIP

If you should be in coverage but are not connected or when you get off the airplane, you can re-establish your connections by pulling down the Notification screen and either tapping the Wi-Fi icon at the top or turning off Airplane mode.

Accessing Mobile (or Not) Websites

The browser on your phone is designed to work like the browser on your PC. At any time, you can enter a web address (URL) by tapping the text box at the top of the screen. You can try this by typing in the address of your favorite website and seeing what happens.

For example, the page shown in Figure 7-2 is the regular version of the website Refdesk.com.

FIGURE 7-2:
The regular version of the website Refdesk.com.

As you can see, the website is all there. Also as you can see, the text is very small. This particular website is designed to take you to a lot of useful links throughout the Internet, so this is an extreme example of a regular website.

While this text is crisp and bright on your beautiful screen, it is still small. You can stretch and pinch to find the information you need. (*Stretching* and *pinching* are hand movements you can use to enlarge/shrink what you see onscreen, as covered in Chapter 2.) With a little bit of practice, you can navigate your familiar websites with ease.

The other option is to find the mobile version of a website. As a comparison, Figure 7-3 shows the mobile version of Refdesk.com. It has fewer pictures, the text is larger, and the mobile version loads faster— but it's less flashy.

MOBILE REFDESK
Saturday, February 9, 2013

- Site of the Day
- Thought of the Day

- DOW | Gas | Business
- Google Calendar

INTERNET SEARCH:
- Google Search
- MSN Live Search
- Yahoo Search

TOP HEADLINES:
- AP | Reuters
- ABC | CBS | CNN
- FOX | MSNBC | NPR
- NYT | USA Today | Wash. Post

MORE NEWS:
- Google News Headlines
- Yahoo News Headlines
- Business Headlines
- Entertainment Headlines
- Sci/Tech Headlines

FIGURE 7-3:
The mobile version of Refdesk.com.

TECHNICAL STUFF

In the case of RefDesk, you can get to the mobile version by entering **m.refdesk.com** into the text block at the top from the software keyboard. Refdesk.com is far from the only website to offer a mobile version. Many sites —from Facebook to Flickr to Gmail to Wikipedia — offer mobile versions.

So how do you get to the mobile websites? If a website has a mobile version, your phone browser will usually bring it up without your having to do anything. Samsung has gone out of its way to work to make the web experience on the Galaxy S8 phone as familiar as possible to what you experience on your PC.

The most common difference between the address of a mobilized website and a regular one is /mobile.com at the end of the address. For example, the mobile version of Amazon.com is www.amazon.com/mobile.

If your phone doesn't automatically bring up the mobile version of a site for some reason, the simplest way to find it is to search for the desired site along with the term **mobile.** For example, the first option you get from searching for IMDb mobile on your phone is the mobilized website for the Internet Movie Database.

Choosing Your Search Engine

If you tapped one of the icons shown in Figure 7-1, you opened up the browser. Now would be a good time to try some of your favorite websites. Go ahead and tap in a few website addresses and see how they look!

One of the early goals for browsers that work on smartphones was to replicate the experience of using the Internet on a PC. For the most part, the browsers on your phone achieve that goal, even if you probably need to practice your zooming and panning.

One of the key decisions for your browser is which search engine you want as the default. You probably want whatever is the search engine that exists on your desktop PC. The leading options are all really good, but you'll probably be happiest with the search engine that you use the most. If you don't care, feel free to skip to the next section on bookmarks.

1. **From the browser screen, tap the Menu icon.**

    Tapping the Menu icon, the three vertical dots to the right of the website address, brings up the menu options shown in Figure 7-4.

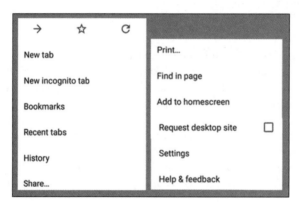

FIGURE 7-4:
The Chrome Menu options.

2. **Tap Settings.**

    Tapping the Settings brings up the screen shown in Figure 7-5.

3. **Tap the Search Engine link.**

    Tapping this setting brings up the screen shown in Figure 7-6.

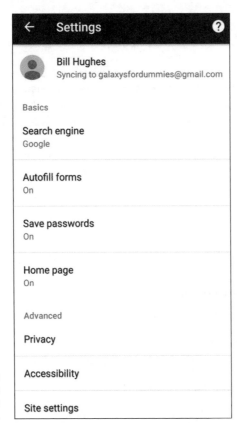

FIGURE 7-5:
The Chrome
Settings
screen.

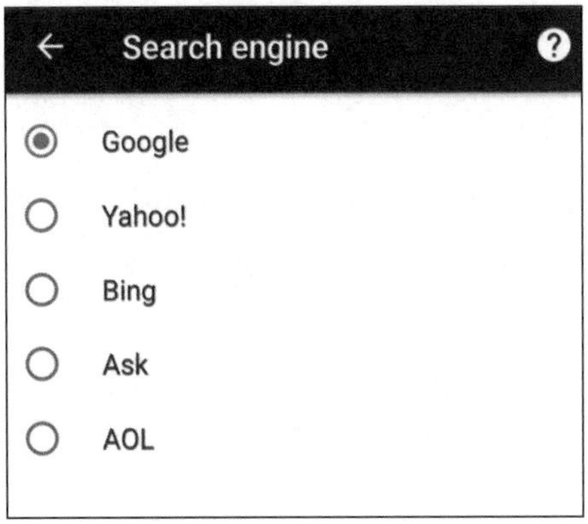

FIGURE 7-6:
The Search
Engine
selections.

4. **Select the search engine you want.**

   Tapping the toggle switch by the name of the search engine you prefer takes care of it all.

Using Bookmarks

As convenient as it is to type URLs or search terms with the keyboard, you'll find it's usually faster to bookmark a web address that you visit frequently. Making bookmarks is a handy way to create a list of favorite sites that you want to access over and over again.

TIP

A *bookmark* is roughly the equivalent of a Favorite on a Microsoft Internet Explorer browser.

Adding bookmarks

When you want to add a website to your bookmark list, simply visit the site. From there, follow these steps:

1. **Tap the Menu options icon.**

This brings up the screen shown earlier in Figure 7-4.

2. **Tap the outline of a star.**

This brings up the screen shown in Figure 7-7.

3. **Decide what to name your bookmark and tap Next.**

The first textbox is the name you want to give to your bookmark. In this case, the default is Conditions & Forecast – WeatherBug.com. You can choose to shorten it to just WeatherBug, or anything you want to call it. When ready, tap Next on the keyboard.

The second textbox is the web address (URL). You probably want to leave this one alone.

4. **Tap the Save button at the bottom-right corner of the screen.**

This puts a thumbnail of the website in your Bookmark file. This is shown in Figure 7-8.

You access this screen through the Menu options shown in Figure 7-4. The next time you come to Bookmarks, you can tap this thumbnail, and this page will refresh and come up in its own window.

FIGURE 7-7:
The Bookmark
screen for your
new addition.

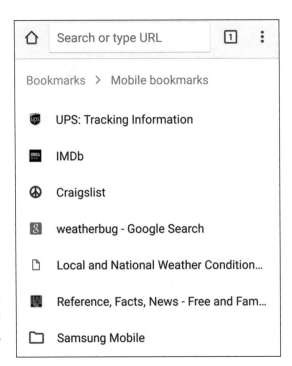

FIGURE 7-8:
The Bookmark
screen with
your new
addition.

Bookmark housekeeping

Bookmarks are cool and convenient, but you don't always want to save them forever. When a bookmark has served its purpose, rather than have it take up prime real estate on your Bookmarks screen, you can delete it. Press and hold the thumbnail of the website you want to delete. Doing so brings up a pop-up like the one shown in Figure 7-9.

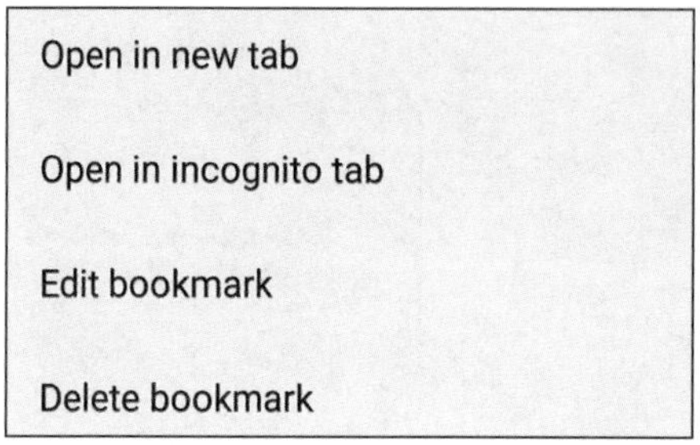

FIGURE 7-9:
Bookmark
housekeeping
options.

> Open in new tab
>
> Open in incognito tab
>
> Edit bookmark
>
> Delete bookmark

To delete a bookmark, tap Delete bookmark. Your phone confirms that this is indeed what you want to do. Tap Yes, and the bookmark is gone.

On the other hand, say you really like this site. You can make it your home page. Tap Set as Homepage. Boom. Done. It's now your home page.

Deciding Between Mobile Browsing and Mobile Apps

When you open the browser, you can use any search engine you want (for example, Bing or Yahoo!). This is a very familiar approach from your experience with PCs. However, you may get very tired of all the pinching and stretching of the screen.

Many companies are aware of this. What they have done is to develop a mobile app that provides you the same information as is available on their website that is formatted for a smartphone screen. Companies in particular will put the information from their website in a mobile app and then add some important mobile features.

For example, it is very convenient to order a custom-made pizza from the website of a national pizza chain. You can order your desired variety of crusts and toppings. The website version also offers directions to the nearest store. The mobile app can take this one step further and give you turn-by-turn directions as you drive to pick up your pizza.

This capability of providing turn-by-turn directions makes no sense for a desktop PC. This capability could make sense for a laptop, but a few laptops have GPS receivers built in. It is also too cumbersome and probably unsafe to rely on turn-by-turn directions from a laptop. It is much easier to get turn-by-turn directions over a smartphone.

This is just one example where downloading a mobile app offers a superior experience. The best part is you get to choose what works for you on your Galaxy S8.

» Finding Play Store on your phone

» Seeing what Play Store has to offer

» Downloading and installing Facebook for Android

» Rating and uninstalling apps

Chapter **8**

Playing in Google's Play Store

One of the things that makes smartphones (such as the phones based on the Google Android platform) different from regular mobile phones is that you can download better apps than what comes standard on the phone. Most traditional cellphones come with a few simple games and basic apps. Smartphones usually come with better games and apps. For example, on your Galaxy S8 phone, you get a more sophisticated Contact Manager, an app that can play digital music (MP3s), basic maps, and texting tools.

To boot, you can download even better apps and games for phones based on the Google Android platform. Many apps are available for your Galaxy S8 phone, and that number will only grow over time.

So where do you get all these wonderful apps? The main place to get Android apps is the Google Play Store. You might be happy with the apps that came with your phone, but look into the Play Store and you'll find apps you never knew you needed and suddenly won't be able to live without.

In this chapter, I introduce you to the Google Play Store and give you a taste of what you find there.

Exploring the Play Store: The Mall for Your Phone

The Play Store is set up and run by Google, mainly for people with Android phones. Adding an app to your phone is similar to adding software to your PC. In both cases, a new app (or software) makes you more productive, adds to your convenience, and/or entertains you for hours on end — sometimes for free. Not a bad deal.

There are some important differences, however, between installing software on a PC and getting an app on a cellphone:

>> **Smartphone apps need to be more stable than computer software because of their greater potential for harm.** If you buy an app for your PC and find that it's unstable (for example, it causes your PC to crash), sure, you'll be upset. If you were to buy an unstable app for your phone, though, you could run up a huge phone bill or even take down the regional cellphone network. Can you hear me now?

>> **There are multiple smartphone platforms.** These days, it's pretty safe to assume that computer software will run on a PC or a Mac or both. On the other hand, because of the various smartphone platforms out there, different versions within a given platform aren't always compatible. The Play Store ensures that the app you're buying will work with your version of phone.

Getting to the Store

You can access the Play Store through your Galaxy S8 phone's Play Store app or through the Internet. The easiest way to access the Play Store is through the Play Store app on your Galaxy S8 phone. The icon is shown in Figure 8-1.

TIP

If the Play Store app isn't already on your Home screen, you can find it in your Apps list. To open it, simply tap the icon.

When you tap the Play Store icon, you're greeted by the screen looking something like what is shown in Figure 8-2.

As new apps become available, the highlighted apps will change, and the Home page will change from one day to the next.

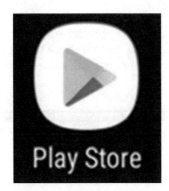

FIGURE 8-1:
The Play Store
icon.

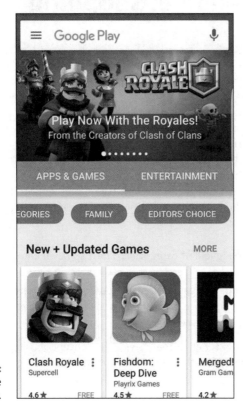

FIGURE 8-2:
The Play Store
home page.

In addition, the good folks at Google spend a lot of time thinking about what is the best way to help the hundreds of millions of Android users find the best application from the selection of 2.7 million apps.

This is no small task. Some of those users are very experienced and know just what they want. Others are walking in the door for the first time while still others are just coming to browse and see whether anything strikes their fancy.

The goal for Google is to make every user who comes in find what they want. The goal in this book is to give you enough information so that you can be comfortable downloading your first app and then comfortable finding other interesting apps as you become more familiar with the layout.

Seeing What's Available: Shopping for Android Apps

The panorama that exists for the Google Play home page seen in Figure 8-2 of is very extensive. You can swipe to the right a long way and you can swipe down dozens of levels. Take a look at the structure of Figure 8-2.

TIP

Do not be surprised if you open up the Play Store home page one day and find that it has a completely different layout. Google tries different formats from time to time to solve one problem or another and keep things fresh. The chances are good that the lower level categories are still there, and you can find what you are looking for, even if the structure described in this chapter is no longer exactly accurate.

Figure 8-2 shows three levels of categories. The Top Level categories are

>> **Apps & Games:** Apps and games are files you download where you are an active participant in their use. These files can be for productivity, information, social connection, or enjoyment.

>> **Movies, Music, Books:** Rather than having the concept of using, this group involves downloading files that entertain or educate you as a passive recipient.

This distinction may seem a little theoretical at this point, but hang in there. An example may help things become clearer.

Say that you want to listen to The Beatle's *White Album* later today on the bus home. You can buy the album in the Entertainment area of the Play Store. When you are on the bus, you could use the Play Music app that came with your phone to bring up and play the *White Album*.

Say that the app Play Music does not do it for you. You can download 103 free music apps and pay for another 132 that allow you to listen to music. You may ask, "Why you would pay for something that you already have for free?" Good question.

Some music apps have a more sophisticated filing system for your music, which is handy if you have a large music library. Others give you an equalizer that increases the bass notes. Another one gives you exciting visuals on the screen that corresponds with the music. Beside, these cost only a dollar or two. There are no judgments here. Buy and use what you like.

Getting back to the original point, you buy the music player app in the Apps and Games Section to play the music and the music file for the *White Album* in Entertainment, which is essentially unchanged since 1968.

Subcategories for Apps and Games

Once you have decided that you want to look at Apps and Games, you see the following options when you tap the link:

>> **Top Charts:** These are the best-selling apps. This is often a good indication that you may want to give it a try.

>> **Games:** These are all the types and flavors of games that can run on your phone, from simple kids games, exotic multiplayer games with alternative realities, and every kind of challenge in between.

>> **Categories:** This option takes you to a hierarchy of application types that is useful if you already know what you want to add. There is more on these different categories later in this chapter.

>> **Family:** If you're looking for apps suitable for the kids, you can go here.

>> **Editors' Choice:** While relying on sales volumes in Top Charts is one way to find apps you may find valuable, this section is curated, hopefully with people who think like you.

Subcategories for Entertainment

There are lots and lots of options for entertainment in this section. They are categorized as follows:

>> **Movies and TV:** As with music, you can download multimedia files and view your favorite movies and TV shows. You can watch these on your Galaxy S8's screen. More on this in Chapter 12.

>> **Music:** You can buy your digital music at the Play Store. I talk more about buying music in Chapter 12.

>> **Books:** Have you been thinking about getting an e-reader, such as an Amazon Kindle? Before you spend your hard-earned cash on one of these e-readers, take a look at the book library here and see whether you like reading on your phone! If you like the way the Kindle works, both are available as apps you can download and use to access your account on Amazon.com.

>> **Newsstand:** Same idea as with books, only this category is for periodicals.

Curated categories

Below the subcategories are rows of curated categories. These are apps grouped by some expert to present you options in a logical sequence. Figure 8-2 shows New + Updated Games. When you scroll down, you'll find dozens of rows, which include such categories as Must-Have Tools, Lifestyle Apps, and Shopping Apps.

If you find a row that you like, you can start scrolling to the right to see the options within that curated category. Hopefully, the curator thinks like you do and can offer you lots of suggestions. This is particularly handy if you're not sure what you want.

The timeless categories for apps and games

Google is doing its best to get you to find the best app for you among its inventory of hundreds of thousands of choices. Today's version of the Play Store has a link called Categories where you can start digging by app or game type. While the names of these categories evolve slightly over time, the following are descriptions that should help you navigate this particular area:

>> **Games:** Your Galaxy S8 phone takes interactive gaming to a new level. Games in this section of the Play Store fall into the following categories:

- *Arcade and Action:* Think of games that are based on what you find in arcades: shooting games, racing games, and other games of skill and/or strategy.

- *Brain and Puzzle:* Think crossword puzzles, Sudoku, and other word or number games.

- *Cards and Casino:* Find an electronic version of virtually every card or casino game. (If you know of any game that's missing, let me know so that I can write the app and sell it to the three people who play it.)

- *Casual:* This crossover category includes simpler games, some of which are also arcade, action, or cards, but are distinguished by the ease with which you can pick them up, play them, and then put them down. Solitaire may be the most widespread example of a casual game.

» **Apps:** The non-games fall into many subcategories:

- *Comics:* These apps are meant to be funny. Hopefully, you find something that tickles your funny bone.

- *Communication:* Yes, the Galaxy S8 phone comes with many communications apps, but these Play Store apps enhance what comes with the phone — for example, tools that automatically send a message if you're running late to a meeting or text you if your kids leave a defined area.

- *Entertainment:* Not games per se, but these apps are still fun: trivia, horoscopes, and frivolous noisemaking apps. (These also include Chuck Norris facts. Did you know that Chuck Norris can divide by 0?)

- *Finance:* This is the place to find mobile banking apps and tools to make managing your personal finances easier.

- *Health:* This is a category for all apps related to mobile medical apps, including calorie counters, fitness tracking, and tools to help manage chronic conditions, such as diabetes.

- *Lifestyle:* This category is a catchall for apps that involve recreation or special interests, like philately or bird-watching.

- *Maps & Search:* Many apps tell you where you are and how to get to where you want to go. Some are updated with current conditions, and others are based on static maps that use typical travel times.

- *Multimedia:* The Galaxy S8 phone comes with the music and video services, but nothing says you have to like them. You might prefer offerings that are set up differently or have a selection of music that isn't available elsewhere.

- *News & Weather:* You'll find a variety of apps that allow you to drill down till you get just the news or weather that's more relevant to you than what's available on your extended Home screen.

- *Productivity:* These apps are for money management (such as a tip calculator), voice recording (such as a stand-alone voice recorder), and time management (for example, an electronic to-do list).

- *Reference:* These apps include a range of reference books, such as dictionaries and translation guides. Think of this section as similar to the reference section of your local library and bookstore.

- *Shopping:* These apps help you with rapid access to mobile shopping sites or do automated comparison shopping.

- *Social:* These are the social networking sites. If you think you know them all, check here just to be sure. Of course, you'll find Facebook, LinkedIn, Twitter, and Pinterest, but you'll also find dozens of other sites that are more narrowly focused and offer apps for the convenience of their users.

- *Software Libraries:* Computers of all sizes come with software libraries to take care of special functions, such as tools to manage ringtones, track app performance, and protect against malware.

- *Sports:* You can find sports sites to tell you the latest scores and analyses in this part of the Play Store.

- *Themes:* Your phone comes with color schemes or *themes.* This part of the Play Store offers a broader selection.

- *Tools:* Some of these are widgets that help you with some fun capabilities. Others are more complicated and help you get more functionality from your phone.

- *Travel:* These apps are useful for traveling, including handy items, such as currency translations and travel guides.

TIP

Many of your favorite websites are now offering apps that are purpose-built for your phone. Chapter 7 talks about how you can access websites on your phone. You can use the full site with your high-resolution screen or use the mobile version. A third alternative can be an app that makes the information you want from your phone even easier to access.

Each app category comes with the apps divided into the following categories:

>> **Top Free:** All apps in the Top Free category are available at no charge.

>> **Top New Free:** This option gets you out in front of the curve to find the best new free apps before the unwashed masses find them.

>> **Top Paid:** All apps in this category charge a fee.

>> **Top Grossing:** These apps are both popular and cost money. This is often a good indication that the app is really good, or at least that it has a crack marketing team. (If the app is not good, the customer comments will show that right away.)

>> **Top New Paid:** All apps in this category charge a fee and are also new.

>> **Trending:** Our friends at Google show the apps that are catching on. It's worth considering the apps that reside in this category.

>> **Featured:** These apps are relatively new and might or might not charge you to download and use them.

In general, you'll probably want to see what you get with a free app before you spend money on the commercial equivalent. Many software companies know this and offer a lower-feature version for free and an enhanced version for a charge. Enjoy the free-market mechanisms on this site and never feel regret for enjoying a free app.

TIP

Free apps are great. But don't be afraid of buying any apps that you're going to use frequently. Apps usually cost very little, and the extra features may be worth it. Some people (including me) have an irrational resistance to paying $1.99 monthly for something they use all the time. Frankly, this is a little silly. Let's all be rational and be willing to pay a little bit for the services we use.

Installing and Managing an Android App

To make the process of finding and downloading an app less abstract, I show you how to download and install one in particular as an example: the Facebook for Android app.

Downloading the Facebook app

Follow these steps to add this app:

1. **Tap the Play Store icon.**

2. **In the Query box, type Facebook.**

   Doing so brings up a drop-down screen like the one shown in Figure 8-3.

   As you can see in the search results, several options include the word Facebook. The other lines in the Apps section are for apps that include the word Facebook. These are typically for apps that enhance Facebook in their own ways — as of this moment, 112,160 of them. Rather than go through these one by one, stick with the one with the Facebook icon.

3. **Tap the anywhere in the box with the Facebook logo.**

   When you tap the box, it brings up the screen shown in Figure 8-4.

FIGURE 8-3:
The Facebook
Search results.

FIGURE 8-4:
The Facebook
app screen in
panorama.

Before continuing to the next step, I want to point out some important elements on this page:

- **Title Line:** The top section has the formal name of the app just above the green Install button. After you click this to download and install the app, you see some other options. I give some examples later in this chapter.

- **Description:** This tells you what the app does.

- **What's New:** This information is important if you have a previous version of this app. Skip this section for now.

- **Screen Captures:** These representative screens are a little too small to read, but they do add some nice color to the page.

- **Feedback Statistics:** This particular app has about 4.0 stars out of 5. That's not bad at all. The other numbers tell you how many folks have voted, how many have downloaded this app, the date it was released, and the size of the app in MB.

- **All Reviews:** This section gets into more details about what people thought of the app beyond the star ranking.

- **More by Facebook:** The app developer in this case is Facebook. If you like the style of a particular developer, this section tells you what other apps that developer offers.

- **Similar Apps:** Just in case you are not sure about this, the good folks at Google offer some alternatives.

- **Users Also Installed:** Play Store tells you the names of other apps downloaded by the customers who downloaded this app. It's a good indicator of what else you may like.

- **Developer:** This section gives you contact information for the developer of this app.

- **Google Play Content:** This is how you tell the Play Store whether this app is naughty or nice.

4. **Tap the dark green button that says Install.**

   You see the progress of the app downloading process. When the app is all there, it begins the installation process.

   At some point in the process, most apps give you a pop-up to let you know what information from your phone that the app will use. This is to give you an idea on how this particular app may affect your privacy.

   Facebook is a special case when it comes to permissions. It touches practically every capability on your phone. Its extensive permission screen is seen in Figure 8-5.

FIGURE 8-5:
The Facebook
permissions
screen.

Most apps are not as intimately connected to your life. These involve far fewer permissions. Some involve only one. For example, Figure 8-6 shows the permissions pop-up for the WeatherBug app. As the name implies, WeatherBug tells you of weather conditions and forecasts. It works best when it knows where you are.

FIGURE 8-6:
The Weather-
Bug permis-
sions pop-up.

Chapter 1 discusses the option to prevent an app from having access to your location information. I mention that you can allow apps to know where you are on a case-by-case basis. Here is where that issue comes up. Each app asks you for permission to access information, such as your location. If you don't want the app to use that information or share it somehow, here's where you find out whether the app uses this information. You may be able to limit the amount of location information. If you're not comfortable with that, you should decline the app in its entirety.

However, in the case of WeatherBug, you can manually enter the location for which you want whether status and forecasts. Each app will let you know what it uses. It is your choice whether you Allow or Deny access.

TIP

This is similar to the license agreements you sign when installing software on your PC. Hopefully, you read them all in detail and understand all the implications. In practice, you hope that it's not a problem if lots of other people have accepted these conditions. In the case of a well-known app like Facebook, you're probably safe, but you should be careful with less-popular apps.

After the app downloads and installs, you will come back to a screen like the one in Figure 8-7.

FIGURE 8-7:
The Play Store app screen for a successfully downloaded app.

5. **Tap the dark green Open button.**

   This brings up the Home screen for Facebook, as shown in Figure 8-8.

   If you have a Facebook account already, go ahead and enter your information. Things will look very familiar. If you don't have a Facebook account, and you want to add one now, go on to the next section.

In any case, the Facebook icon appears on your Apps screen along with some other recently added apps, such as Angry Birds and Solitaire. This is seen in Figure 8-9.

REMEMBER

If you want this app to be on your Home screen, press and hold the icon. The Facebook icon appears on your Home screen.

FIGURE 8-8:
The Facebook
login screen.

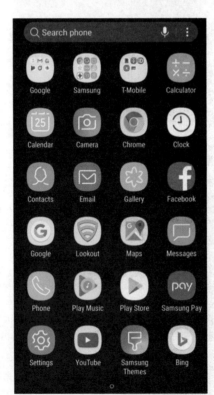

FIGURE 8-9:
The Facebook
icon on the
Apps screen.

Creating a Facebook account

If you don't already have a Facebook account, you can create an account here. Toward the bottom of the screen is the option to sign up for Facebook. Tap the Sign Up for Facebook link, and you see the screen shown in Figure 8-10.

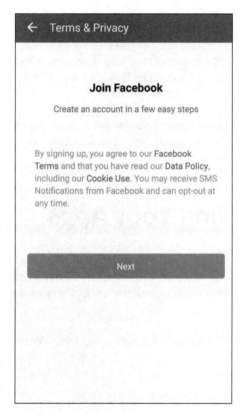

FIGURE 8-10:
The Sign Up for Facebook Home screen.

To sign up for Facebook, you should have the following information:

>> **Name:** This would seem to be simple question. However, you should consider adding former names and/or nicknames. This all depends upon whether you want to be found by old friends or not.

>> **Mobile number:** Your mobile telephone number will auto-populate for this question. You may want to use another number. Your choice.

>> **Your birthday:** Go ahead. Tell the truth on this one.

>> **Your password:** Pick one that you can remember.

>> **Your gender:** I am not sure why Facebook needs to know this, but pick one gender.

After you enter this information, Facebook sends a verification message. If you provide an email address, the app sends you an email. If you use your mobile phone number, it sends you a text.

The email or text contains a code. Enter this code, and your Facebook account is validated. To get the most out of Facebook, I recommend checking out *Facebook For Dummies,* 6th Edition (John Wiley & Sons, Inc.) by Carolyn Abram.

Within the Facebook app itself, you see the latest posts from your friends in an instant. You get your daily serving of cute kitten images, stories from proud parents about their children, and messages from old flames wondering about what might have been.

TIP

The Facebook mobile app is pretty popular with users. According to Facebook, more than half of Facebook users only use their smartphones and never bother to check their posts on a PC!

Rating or Uninstalling Your Apps

Providing feedback to an app is an important part of maintaining the strength of the Android community. It's your responsibility to rate apps honestly. (Or you can blow it off and just take advantage of the work others have put into the rating system. It's your choice.)

If you want to make your voice heard about an app, here are the steps:

1. **Open the Play Store.**

   Refer to Figure 8-2 to see the layout.

2. **Tap the Menu button (the three parallel lines in the Google Play banner).**

   Doing so brings up a drop-down menu like the one shown in Figure 8-11.

3. **Tap the link that says My Apps & Games.**

   This tap brings up the screen shown in Figure 8-12, which lists all the apps on your phone. Keep on scrolling down. You'll eventually see them all.

Tapping on one of these apps is how you rate them or uninstall them, as shown in Figure 8-13.

If you love the app, rate it highly on a five star scale. To be clear, to rank it as one star, tap the leftmost star. To rank it highly with five stars, tap the rightmost star.

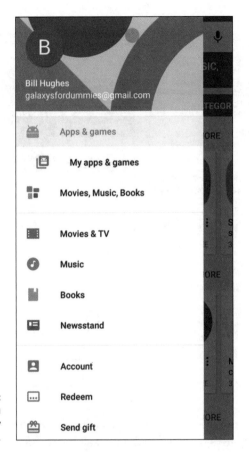

FIGURE 8-11:
The menu
from the Play
Store.

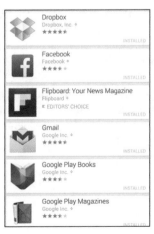

FIGURE 8-12:
The My Apps &
Games screen
in panorama.

Uninstall button

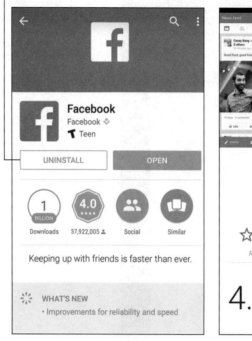 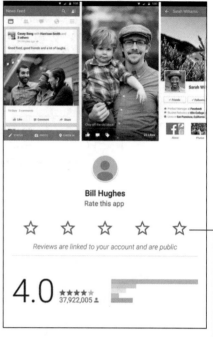

Rating buttons

FIGURE 8-13:
The Apps page
for Facebook
after it is
installed.

Whatever number of stars you pick will bring up a pop-up with those number of stars, as shown in Figure 8-14. You can then tell all the world just what you think of the app.

While many app developers read the comments, it takes longer for some. I am still waiting to hear back from my comments. Please note that seeking bribes to provide positive reviews is entirely my idea, and you should probably not copy this approach. I will sue if you do.

On the other hand, if you hate the app, give it one star and blast away. It does not happen often, but there are some major league loser apps out there. In most cases, it occurs when you have an older phone, and the apps you have assume some capabilities that are not there.

READ MORE

Review by Bill Hughes

★ ★ ★ ★ ☆

Liked it

My opinion is for sale

Good app, but Mark Z. should give me
a few of his billions to give 5 stars. I
am just saying...

SUBMIT

4.0 ★★★★★
37,922,005

FIGURE 8-14:
The Rating
pop-up.

This will not happen for a long, long time with the Galaxy S8, but technology does march on. Someday in the future, your wonderful phone will be a relic, and some new apps will assume that your S8 can be operated through thought control/mind reading. Alas, your S8 phone does not have that feature (as far as you know). The new app will not seem to work right.

Go ahead and give that app one star and then tap the Uninstall button. Poof. It is gone.

4
Having Fun with Your Phone

» **Organizing your pictures and video**

» **Sharing pictures and video with friends and family**

Chapter **9**

Sharing Pictures

The Samsung Galaxy S8 should really be called a smartcamera with a phone. If you're like many mobile phone users, you love that you can shoot photographs and video with your phone.

You probably carry your phone with you practically everywhere you go, so you never again have to miss a great photograph because you left your camera at home.

And don't think that Samsung skimped on the camera on your Galaxy S8. Boasting 16 MP of muscle, this camera is complemented with lots of shooting options. Then, you can view your shots on that wicked Super AMOLED screen. Samsung also includes a Gallery app for organizing and sharing. Plus, the camera can shoot stills *and* video.

It's truly amazing to consider the number of options that you have for your photographs and your videos. Samsung keeps on adding new options, filters, and ways to share these files. It would not be surprising if your phone now has more capabilities than your digital camera.

These capabilities actually cause a problem. There are so many options that it can be overwhelming. Research has shown that people fall into one of three categories: The first group tends to use the default settings. If they want to alter the image, they'd prefer to do it on their own PCs. The second group likes to explore some of the capabilities on the phone and will have some fun looking at the scenarios, but keep things within reason. The third group goes nuts with all the capabilities of the phone.

To accommodate everyone, this chapter starts with the basics. I cover how to use the camera on your phone, view your pictures, and share them online. This works for everybody.

I then focus on the most popular settings for the second group. There are some important capabilities.

For the third group, the best that can be done is to lead you in the right direction. As much as I would like to, it would be impossible to cover all the options and combinations. In my count, there are 2.43 billion possible combinations of filters, lighting, and modes. If you were to start now and take a picture every 10 seconds, you would not run out of combinations for over 700 years. This would not even include all the options for sharing these images.

Realistically, neither you nor your phone will last that long. To keep things in the realm of reality, I introduce only the most important and valuable options and go from there.

Say Cheese! Taking a Picture with Your Phone

Before you can take a picture, you have to open the Camera app. The traditional way is to simply access the Camera application from the Application list. Just tap the Camera icon to launch the app.

Because the camera is so important, here are a few more ways to get to the Camera app. First, press the Power button twice. Boom. There it is.

Next, unless you have turned off the capability for security purposes, there is a camera icon on your lock screen. If you swipe the icon across the screen, the Camera app bypasses the security setting. You can snap away, but you can't access the photo gallery or any other files.

TIP

Here is a suggestion. If you see something suspicious, but are not ready to call 911, go ahead and start taking photos of what concerns you. If you need to, you can go back to the lock screen and slide the phone icon to the right to call 911, again without needing to unlock.

A closely related application on your phone is the Gallery, which is where your phone stores your images. The icons for these two apps are shown in the margin.

Gallery

With the Camera app open, you're ready to take a picture within a second or two. The screen becomes your viewfinder. You see a screen like the one shown in Figure 9-1.

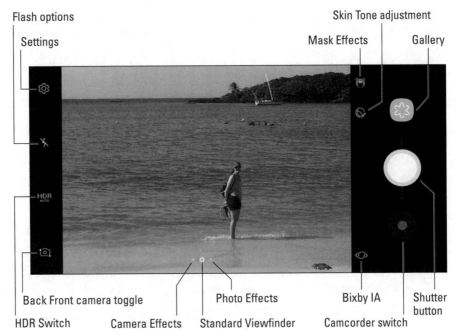

Flash options

Settings

Skin Tone adjustment

Mask Effects

Gallery

FIGURE 9-1:
The screen is
the viewfinder
for the Camera
app.

Back Front camera toggle

HDR Switch   Camera Effects   Standard Viewfinder

Photo Effects

Bixby IA   Shutter
                    button

Camcorder switch

And how do you snap the picture? Just tap the big white button on the right, which is the digital shutter button. The image in your viewfinder turns into a digital image.

This screen still uses a significant share of battery life, but less than with earlier technologies. With Super AMOLED, you even save more power if you use darker backgrounds where possible. A few picture-taking options are right there on the viewfinder. Going clockwise from the upper-right corner, the options include

>> **Gallery:** Tap this icon to take you to see the pictures you have just taken. I discuss the Gallery in the section "Managing Your Photo Images," later in this chapter.

>> **Shutter control:** This icon takes the picture.

>> **Camera/Video camera switch:** This icon takes you from the camera to the video camera.

>> **Bixby:** Bixby can do some cool things with your image. It can tell you what you're looking at. If you know what it is and want to buy it, Bixby can tell you how much it is at other retailers. More about Bixby in Chapter 14.

A SUPER-FAST PRIMER ON SUPER AMOLED

All Samsung Galaxy S8 phones have a Super AMOLED screen. Allow me to take a moment to explain what makes this so good — and what makes you so smart for having bought the Samsung Galaxy S8.

To start, think about a typical LCD screen, like what your TV or PC might have. LCDs are great, but they work best indoors where it's not too bright. LCDs need a backlight (fluorescent, most commonly), and the backlight draws a fair amount of power, although much less power than a CRT. When used on a phone, an LCD screen is the largest single user of battery life, using more power than the radios or the processor. Also, because of the backlight on an LCD screen, these screens display black as kinda washed-out, not a true black.

The next step has been to use light-emitting diodes (LEDs), which convert energy to light more efficiently. Monochrome LEDs have been used for decades. They are also used in the mongo-screens (jumbotrons) in sports arenas. Until recently, getting the colors right was a struggle. (Blue was a big problem.) That problem was solved by using organic materials (*organic* as in carbon-based, as opposed to being grown with no pesticides) for LEDs.

The first organic LEDs (OLEDs) looked good, drew less power, and offered really dark blacks, but still had two problems. Their imaging really stank in bright light, even worse than did LCD screens. Also, there was a problem with *crosstalk* — individual pixels would get confused, over time about whether they were on or off. You'd see green or red pixels remaining on-screen, even if the area was clearly supposed to be dark. It was very distracting.

The solution to the pixels' confusion is called *Active Matrix,* which tells the pixels more frequently whether they are to be on or off. When you have Active Matrix technology, you have an Active Matrix Organic LED, or AMOLED. The image you get with this technology still stinks in bright light, but at least it's some improvement.

Enter the Super AMOLED technology, made by Samsung. When compared with the first AMOLED screens, Super AMOLED screens are 20 percent brighter, use 20 percent less power, and cut sunlight reflection by 80 percent. This is really super!

>> **Photo Effects:** You can do some fancy things to enhance the image. We explore the options later in the "Effects options" section.

>> **The viewfinder:** The viewfinder shows what will be in the picture. Okay. This is obvious, but this is also how you control the magnification. From within the

viewfinder, you can zoom in and out by pinching or stretching the screen. See Figure 9-2 for an example.

- Stretch the screen to zoom in.

- Pinch the screen to zoom out.

FIGURE 9-2:
The viewfinder
when zooming.

>> **Camera Effects:** These are some of the cool things you get when you have a high-resolution camera combined with super-fast processing. This includes support for panorama images, a slow-motion camera, and tools to specifically enhance images of food. More on this later in the chapter.

>> **Rear facing camera to front-facing camera switch:** This icon takes you from the 12 megapixel (MP) rear-facing camera to the not-too-shabby 5 MP front-facing camera. This is a good option for selfies as you can see what the shot will look like before you snap it.

>> **HDR switch:** Your phone can automatically compensate when the light sources add a blue or red tint. You do this by having the HDR in Auto mode. You can also remove this capability, but why?

>> **Flash options:** Even if you want to keep it simple, you'll want to know how to control your flash. Sometimes you need a flash for your photo. Sometimes you need a flash for your photo, but it's not allowed, as when you're taking images of fish in an aquarium, newborns, or some animals. (Remember what

happened to King Kong?) Regardless of the situation, your phone gives you control of the flash. Tap the Settings icon at the top of the viewfinder. You have the options of Off, On, or Auto Flash, which lets the light meter within the camera decide whether a flash is necessary. The options are shown in Figure 9-3.

The Galaxy S8 will figure out if a flash is needed

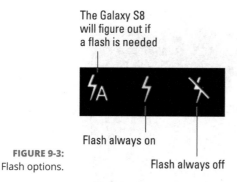

Flash always on

FIGURE 9-3:
Flash options.

Flash always off

>> **Settings:** Settings also gives some fancy options that are covered in the next section.

>> **Mask Effect:** This option lets you put bunny ears on your selfie. You can put cute masks on you, your friends, or your worst enemies.

>> **Skin tone adjustment:** You can use this option to clean up some blemishes on your pictures in real-time.

TIP

You probably know that it's not a good idea to touch the lens of a camera. At the same time, it's practically impossible to avoid touching the lenses on your Galaxy S8. This can create a problem where there can be a buildup of oil and dirt on your high-resolution lens. You should clean the lens of your camera from time to time with a microfiber cloth to get the most out of your camera. Otherwise, your high-resolution images might look like you live in a perpetual fog bank.

After you take a picture, you have a choice. The image is automatically stored in another application: the Gallery. This allows you to keep on snapping away and come back to the Gallery when you have time. I cover the Gallery application more in the upcoming section "Managing Your Photo Images."

FOR SKEPTICS ONLY

If you've ever used a cameraphone, you might be thinking, "Why make such a big deal about this camera's phone? Cameraphones aren't worth the megapixels they're made of." Granted, in the past, many cameraphones weren't quite as good as a digital camera, but Samsung has addressed these issues with the Galaxy S8:

- **Resolution:** The resolution on most cameraphones was lower than what you typically get on a dedicated digital camera. The Galaxy S8, however, sports a 12 megapixel (MP) camera — and that's good enough to produce an 8-x-10-inch print that's indistinguishable from what you could produce with a film camera, and 4 x 6-inch photos are plenty large for most uses.

- **Low Light:** Many cameraphones perform badly in low light conditions. The Galaxy S8 has an f/1.4 lens, which will impress the folks who know what that means. The implication is that the S8 works incredibly well in low light.

- **AutoFocus:** We amateurs like it when a camera will do the hard work of focusing. The technology in the S8 takes a big leap by having more pixels figuring out where to focus.

- **Photo transfer:** With most cameraphones, the photos are hard to move from the camera to a computer. With the Samsung Galaxy S8, however (remember: it uses the Android operating system), you can quickly and easily send an image, or a bunch of images, anywhere you want, easily and wirelessly.

- **Screen resolution:** In practice, many cameraphone users just end up showing their pictures to friends right on their phones. Many cameraphone screens, however, don't have very good resolution, which means your images don't look so hot when you want to show them off to your friends. The good news is that the Samsung Galaxy S8 has a bright, high-resolution screen. Photos look really good on the Super AMOLED screen.

- **Organization:** Most cameraphones don't offer much in the way of organizational tools. Your images are all just there on your phone, without any structure. But the Samsung Galaxy S8 has the Gallery application that makes organizing your photos easier. It's also set up to share these photos easily.

However, if you want to send that image right away, here's what you do:

1. **From the viewfinder screen, tap the Gallery icon.**

   The viewfinder shows the Gallery icon at the top-right corner of the viewfinder. When you tap it, it brings up the Gallery application, as shown in Figure 9-4.

   This brings up the current image, along with the some other recent photos.

FIGURE 9-4:
The Gallery
app.

2. **Tap the thumbnail of the image you want to share.**

It also brings up some options, as seen in Figure 9-5. Right now, you're interested in the Share option.

FIGURE 9-5:
Gallery options
for the current
image.

Bixby Vision   Auto adjust   Share   Edit   Delete

3. **Tap the Share button.**

This brings up the options you can use to forward the image; see Figure 9-5 (although your phone might not support all the options listed here and may have a few others not in this image).

- **Messaging:** This allows you to send it immediately to someone's phone as a text message.

- **Bluetooth:** Send images to devices, such as a laptop or phone, linked with a Bluetooth connection.

- **Photos:** Google Photos, formerly known as Picasa, is a website created to help its subscribers organize and share photos. The main advantage for subscribers is that they can send links to friends or family for them to see a thumbnail of images, rather than sending a large number of high-resolution files. Read more on Google Photos in the next section.

- **Email:** Send the image as an attachment with your primary email account.

- **Facebook:** You can take a picture and post it on your Facebook account with this option.

- **Gmail:** If your main email is with Gmail, this option and the Email option are the same.

- **Your cloud provider:** Figure 9-6 shows Goggle Drive, but if you sign up for any of the cloud storage options, they'll be here.

- **Wi-Fi Direct:** Talk about slick! This option turns your phone into a Wi-Fi access point so that your Wi-Fi–enabled PC or another smartphone can establish a connection with you.

The point is that there is an overabundance of options. If an app on your device works with images, this is the place you can upload that image. If one of these options doesn't quite suit your need to share your pictures, perhaps you're being too picky!

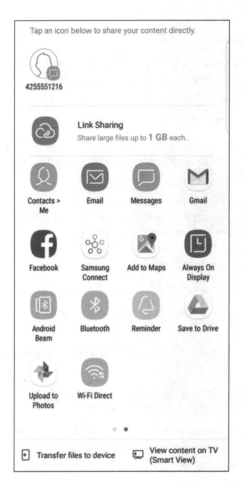

FIGURE 9-6:
Sharing options for the current image.

Getting a Little Fancier with Your Camera

Using the default Camera settings to snap pics is perfectly fine for those can-did, casual, on-the-go shots — say, friends in your living room. However, your Samsung Galaxy S8 phone camera can support much more sophisticated shots. Your digital SLR camera has a bigger lens than your phone, but I can assure you that your phone has a much bigger brain than your camera. I suggest that even the users who want these default settings get familiar with the camera's Mode set-tings. These are easy to access and will improve the image quality with minimal effort.

The Camera Effects settings

The Mode setting is where you make some basic settings that describe the situation under which you will be taking your shot. The default is a single picture in Automatic mode. The Camera Effects icon is the leftmost round dot toward the bottom of the viewfinder.

Sliding this icon to the right brings up the options shown in Figure 9-7.

FIGURE 9-7:
The Camera
Effects options
on the camera
viewfinder.

Tapping the Mode icon brings up a number of choices:

>> **Auto:** Taking a single photo at a time is the default setting, which assumes average light. It's a good place to start.

>> **Pro:** This mode gets you to all kinds of camera settings that someone who knows what he or she is doing would want to control rather than let the camera make the choice. This includes setting the exposure, shutter speed, ISO sensitivity, white balance, focal length, and color tone. If you do not know what these mean, this is not the mode for you.

>> **Panorama:** This setting lets you take a wider shot than you can with a single shot. Press the Camera button while you rotate through your desired field of view. The application then digitally stitches the individual photos into a single wide-angle shot.

>> **Selective focus:** This setting lets you get within 20 inches of an object, which is too close for the normal autofocus. On top of that, you can change the focus after taking the photo. (You read that right!)

>> **Slow motion:** This switches you to video mode to slow down really fast shots.

- » **Hyperlapse:** You can use this setting to create a time-lapse video. The video camera will adjust the speed of the shots based upon the movement of the phone.

- » **Food:** This takes pictures that emphasize the colors in food to make your friends even more jealous (and/or hungry).

- » **Virtual shot:** Put an image in the viewfinder and walk around it. The phone figures out where you are and creates a virtual tour. If this does not prove to you that your phone is a "smarticle," nothing will.

Choose the option that sounds right and snap away.

Settings options on the viewfinder

Tapping the Settings icon on the viewfinder brings up a number of choices. This list gives you control of the rear camera (the one with higher resolution), the front-facing camera, which is used for selfies or video-calls, and settings that affect both cameras. These options are shown in Figure 9-8:

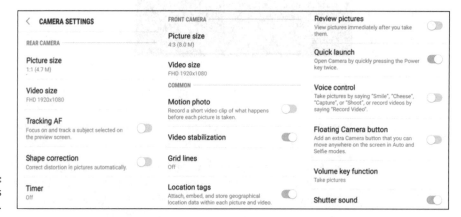

FIGURE 9-8: The Settings options.

- » **Picture size:** One option is to pick the highest resolution and take all your images at that setting. That would be 12 megapixels per picture. Another option is to pick the lowest resolution so you can take more pictures with a given size of storage. That would be 4.7 megapixels per picture. Probably the best option is to figure out what you plan to do with the pictures and then decide the lowest resolution that will work. If all you're going to do is put the pictures on Facebook, all that will happen is that this website will discard most of the pixels after you spent your time and money uploading high-resolution pictures. The best advice is to experiment with different resolutions and use the ones that best meet your needs. As seen in Figure 9-9, you can set the rear-facing and the front-facing camera at different resolutions.

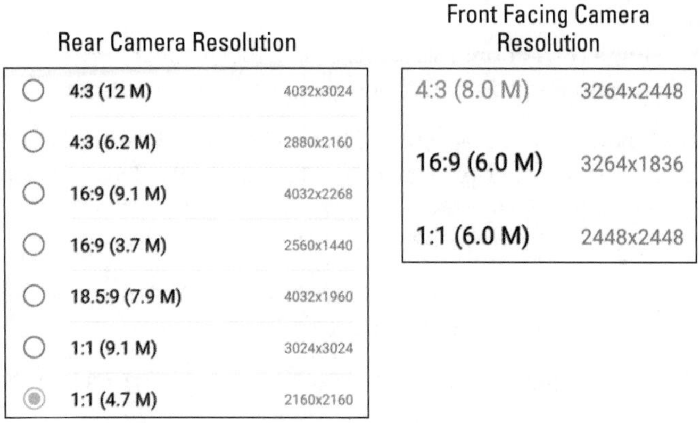

Rear Camera Resolution

Front Facing Camera Resolution

○	4:3 (12 M)	4032x3024
○	4:3 (6.2 M)	2880x2160
○	16:9 (9.1 M)	4032x2268
○	16:9 (3.7 M)	2560x1440
○	18.5:9 (7.9 M)	4032x1960
○	1:1 (9.1 M)	3024x3024
◉	1:1 (4.7 M)	2160x2160

4:3 (8.0 M)	3264x2448
16:9 (6.0 M)	3264x1836
1:1 (6.0 M)	2448x2448

FIGURE 9-9: Your phone's image resolution options for rear- and front-facing cameras.

>> **Video size:** You have the option to get really carried away here. The lowest video option is VGA. This is the resolution of your old, analog television. That was perfectly adequate for us for many decades, but HD is the minimally acceptable resolution for thoroughly modern folks. However, your phone scoffs at this puny resolution, and can take it to four higher settings, as seen in Figure 9-10. The only reason to hesitate to use these higher settings is that, just as with still pictures, videos recorded in higher resolutions take more memory. It is good to know these resolutions are there. In addition to higher resolution, the FHD (60 fps) steps up quality by taking many more images per second. FHD normally uses between 24 and 30 frames per second. Using 60 frames per second removes any flicker at all. It also uses twice the amount of memory.

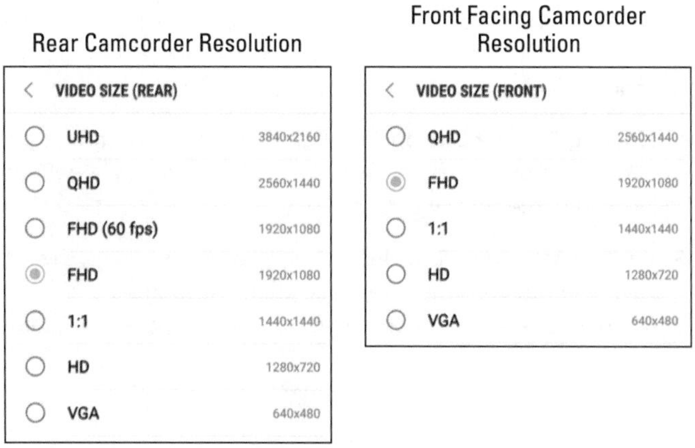

Rear Camcorder Resolution

Front Facing Camcorder Resolution

‹ VIDEO SIZE (REAR)		
○	UHD	3840x2160
○	QHD	2560x1440
○	FHD (60 fps)	1920x1080
◉	FHD	1920x1080
○	1:1	1440x1440
○	HD	1280x720
○	VGA	640x480

‹ VIDEO SIZE (FRONT)		
○	QHD	2560x1440
◉	FHD	1920x1080
○	1:1	1440x1440
○	HD	1280x720
○	VGA	640x480

FIGURE 9-10: Your phone's camcorder resolution options for rear and front-facing cameras.

» **Tracking AF:** The Samsung Galaxy S8 can spot a person's face and assumes that you want it to be the place where you focus if you toggle this option to the On position. Otherwise, if you don't use this mode, the camera may assume that you want whatever is in the center of the viewfinder to be in focus.

» **Shape correction:** This sophisticated tool automatically takes care of any distortions in objects that you sometimes see in pictures.

» **Timer:** The front-facing camera is meant for selfies, but sometimes you want to use the higher-resolution, rear-facing camera. You can use the timer to set up a delay of a few seconds between the time you tap the shutter release and the time the camera takes the shot.

» **Motion photo:** This is a neat capability. Selecting this option records a short video clip before you take the still photo.

» **Video stabilization:** If too much caffeine is causing your shots to blur, this capability is your answer.

» **Grid lines:** Some people like to have a 3 x 3 grid on the viewfinder to help frame the shot. If you are one of these people, toggle on this option.

» **Location tags:** The Samsung Galaxy S8 uses its GPS to tell the location of where you took the shot. If this is too intrusive, you can leave out this information on the image description.

» **Review pictures:** Some people want to see the shot right away. Others want to take a bunch of pictures and look at them at their leisure. If you want to see the image right away to see whether you need to take a second picture, turn on this toggle. It will jump you in to the Gallery app right away.

» **Quick launch:** You can launch the camera by pressing the Home button twice. If you would rather not, here is where you can disable that setting.

» **Voice control:** This option lets you turn voice control on. Your camera is listening to you. If you say, "Smile," "Cheese," "Capture," or "Shoot," the camera will snap a shot. This is simpler than using the self-timer. If you say, "Record video," the video recorder will start recording. In either case, you can tell it to zoom by saying "zoom" — or not if you turn off this option.

» **Floating Camera button:** This is not the option to support putting your phone on a drone. This allows you to relocate on the viewfinder screen the location of the shutter button. Sorry.

» **Volume keys function:** This setting allows, or disables, the increase/decrease volume buttons on the side of the phone to control the shutter, the video recorder, or the zoom/pan capability when in camera or video mode.

>> **Shutter sound:** It can be satisfying to hear the click when you take a picture. If you would rather not, turn that sound off here.

>> **Reset settings:** If you mess something up, tap Reset settings, and it will take you back to the default settings.

Photo Effects options

When you slide the rightmost dot within the viewfinder to the left, you get to see a number of effects that you can apply to your image. Some examples are shown in Figure 9-11.

FIGURE 9-11: Some examples of Effects options.

Select the option that looks right for your creative vision by tapping on the thumbnail and snap away.

The Digital Camcorder in Your Pocket

Your Samsung Galaxy S8 Camera application can also function as a digital camcorder.

Starting the camcorder

All you need to do to use your phone as a video recorder is to put your camera into Camcorder mode. From the camera viewfinder, you tap the icon that looks like the record button of a movie camera in the upper-right corner, and you switch from photographer to videographer.

 At this point, recording video automatically starts. You get the notification that says "Rec" in red and the timer from when it started.

The recording continues until you either tap the stop button, which is the circle with the dark square in the center on the right side of the viewfinder (see Figure 9-12), or the pause button, which is the button with the parallel slashes in the middle. If you press the stop button, the screen will revert back to the still camera.

FIGURE 9-12:
Your phone's
camcorder
viewfinder.

If you press the pause button while in camcorder mode, the buttons to the right morph into the options seen in the small image below it. You can tap the upper button to switch back to the camera. Your other option is to tap the button with the red dot to begin recording again.

 Your phone is not only recording the video; it's also recording the sound. Be careful what you say!

REMEMBER

Taking and sharing videos with your camcorder

Just as you share photos you take with the camera, you can immediately share a video, play it, or delete it by tapping the video viewer. Also, the video is immediately saved on your camera. It's stored in the Gallery app or is viewable from your Video Player app (see Chapter 12).

You can get fancy with some of the settings for your camcorder, but you won't find nearly as many settings as you have for your camera (fortunately!). Two settings: AF and brightness. AF lets you changes where you want the camera to use its autofocus. The default for automatic focusing is to assume that you want whatever is smack-dab in the center of the screen to be in most focus. However, sometimes you may want to get fancy with framing the shot, and focus on your family in the bottom part of the image with Mount Rushmore taking up most of the screen. In this case, you tell the camera to autofocus on the lower part of the screen and do its best on the rest of the image. Brightness lets you adjust the brightness of the video. Otherwise, it's all automatic.

Managing Your Photo Images

After you take some great pictures, you need to figure out what to do with them. Although you can send an image immediately to another site or via email, it will likely be the exception.

In most cases, it's easier to keep on doing what you were doing and go back to the Gallery application when you have some time to take a look at the images and then decide what to do with them. Your choices include

>> Store them on your phone within the Gallery app.

>> Transfer them to your PC to your photo album application by sending them with email.

>> Store them on an Internet site, like Google Photo or Flickr.

>> Print them from your PC.

>> Email or text them to your friends and family.

>> Any combination of the preceding choices.

Unlike many regular phones with a built-in camera, the Galaxy S8 makes it easy to access these choices. You need to determine the approach you want to take to keep your images when you want them to stick around. The rest of this chapter goes through your options.

REMEMBER

Even though the Camera application and the Gallery application are closely related, they are two separate apps. Be sure that you keep straight which application you want to use.

The Gallery Home screen (refer to Figure 9-4) shows how the app first sorts the images on your phone into folders, depending upon when they originated.

All your photos from the Camera app are placed in files sorted by date. The application takes a shot at grouping them when a series of pictures or videos are taken about the same time.

Using Images on Your Phone

In addition to sharing photos from your camera, your Galaxy S8 phone allows you to use a Gallery photo as wallpaper or as a photo for a contact. And if the fancy shooting settings in the Camera application aren't enough, you can wrangle minor edits — as in cropping or rotating — when you have an image in the Gallery application.

The first step is to find the image that you want in Gallery. If you want to do something to this image other than send it, tap the Edit button at the bottom of the screen (refer to Figure 9-5). Some of the options include

>> **Slideshow:** This displays each of the images for a few seconds. You can not only set the speed for transition, but also add music and select among several image transitions.

>> **Crop:** Cut away unnecessary or distracting parts of the image. The application creates a virtual box around what it considers to be the main object. You can move the box around the image, but you cannot resize it. You then can either save this cropped image or discard.

>> **Set As:** Make this image your wallpaper or set it as the image for a contact.

>> **Print:** This option allows you to print if you have set up a local printer to communicate with your phone either through Wi-Fi or Bluetooth.

>> **Rename:** These options allow you to rotate the image right or left. This is useful if you turned the camera sideways to get more height in your shot and now want to turn the image to landscape (or vice versa).

>> **Details:** See the information on the image — its metadata, which is fixed and cannot change.

Deleting Images on Your Phone

Not all the images on your phone are keepers. When you want to get rid of an image, press and hold the image you want to delete. In a second, a checkbox with the image selected will appear. Also, the links appear at the top to either Share or Delete. If you want to delete this image, tap Delete. The camera verifies that this is your intent. After you confirm, the image goes away.

If you want to delete more images, you can tap all the images you want to make go away. It is selected if it has a green checkmark on the image. Tap away, then hit delete. It will confirm with you once. Tap again and these images are gone forever.

WARNING

When I say that the photos you delete are gone forever, I do mean *for-ev-er*. Most of us have inadvertently deleted the only copy of an image from a PC or a digital camera. That's not a pleasant feeling, so be careful.

» **Downloading games to your phone**

» **Keeping track of what you've downloaded**

» **Providing feedback**

Chapter **10**

Playing Games

G ames are the most popular kind of download for smartphones of all kinds. In spite of the focus on business productivity, socializing, and making your life simpler, games outpace all other application downloads. To this point, the electronic gaming industry has larger revenues than the movie industry — and has for several years!

The fact of the matter is that your Samsung Galaxy S8, with its large Super AMOLED screen and beefy graphics processing unit, makes Android-based games more fun. And because you already have one, maybe you should take a break and concentrate on having fun!

The Play Store Games Category

Chapter 8 introduces the Play Store, shown in Figure 10-1. The first level categorization split offerings into two categories: Apps & Games and Entertainment. While most of us play games for the purpose of entertainment, the Entertainment section involves options that are created for our passive enjoyment.

We want games. Games that test our skills; games that are fun; games that are cute; games that immerse us in an alternate universe! To get there, tap on the Apps & Games link!

Top-level categories

Google Play Menu button

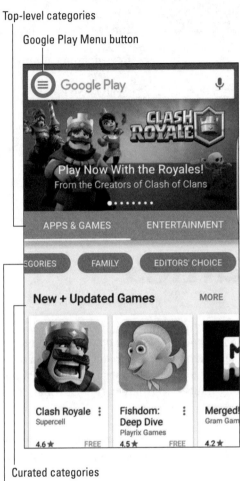

FIGURE 10-1:
The Play Store
Game Home
screen.

Curated categories

Subcategories

We could have a lively and intellectually stimulating debate on the merits of games versus applications. For the purposes of this book, the differences between games and apps are as follows:

>> If a person likes a game, he or she tends to play it for a while, maybe for a few weeks or even months, and then stops using it. A person who likes an app tends to keep on using it.

>> Games tend to use more of the graphical capabilities of your phone.

>> People who use their phones for games tend to like to try a wide range of games.

The Apps & Games section offers tools to help you with fitness, business productivity, and education. Fie, Bah, Boo, I say! Save that for another time. Now you want to have some fun!! Let's go find some good games for your Samsung Galaxy S8.

The best way to approach this is to find the link in the subcategories that says Games. Click on the subcategories, and you will find the Games link, as shown in Figure 10-2.

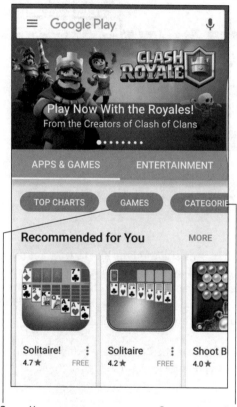

FIGURE 10-2:
The Games link on the Google Play Home screen.

You now go to a section of the store that is nothing but games. This section includes everything from simple puzzles to simulated violence. All games involve various combinations of intellect, skill (either cognitive or motor), and role-playing. Let's do it.

The Games Home screen

When you tap on the Games option shown in Figure 10-2, you go to the Home screen for Games. If you scroll down, you see many suggested games. This is shown in panorama in Figure 10-3.

FIGURE 10-3:
The Games
Home screen
in Panorama.

If you aren't sure what games you might like to try, don't worry: There are lots of options. As you can see, the Home screen makes lots of suggestions. Each row takes a different perspective on helping you find a new game. A few of these are board games, strategy games, and action games. They also include games that allow you to play offline without Wi-Fi.

Another approach is to choose the Categories options, shown in Figure 10-2. This will bring up the game categories shown in Figure 10-4.

All categories

Action	Casino	Role Playing
Adventure	Casual	Simulation
Arcade	Educational	Sports
Board	Music	Strategy
Card	Puzzle	Trivia
	Racing	Word

FIGURE 10-4:
The Games
Categories tab.

The Games Categories tab

If you scroll to the left from the tab that says Home, you see a tab for Categories. These are shown in Figure 10-4.

In the Play Store, games are divided into the following genres:

>> **Action:** Games that involve shooting projectiles that can range from marshmallows to bullets to antiballistic missiles. They also involve fighting games with every level of gore possible.

>> **Adventure:** Games that take you to virtual worlds where you search for treasure and/or fight evil. Zombies and vampires are traditional evildoers.

>> **Arcade:** Game room and bar favorites.

>> **Board:** Versions of familiar (and some not-so-familiar) board games.

>> **Card:** All the standard card games are here.

>> **Casino:** Simulations of gambling games; no real money changes hands.

>> **Casual:** Games that you can easily pick up and put aside (unless you have and addictive personality).

>> **Educational:** Enjoyable games that also offer users enhanced skills or information.

>> **Music:** Includes a wide range of games that involve music in one way or another. These games may include trivia, educational games involving learning music, or sing-a-long songs for kids.

>> **Puzzle:** Includes games like Sudoku, word search, and Trivial Pursuit.

>> **Racing:** Cars, go-karts, snowboards, jet skis, biplanes, jets, or spacecraft competing with one another.

>> **Role Playing:** In a virtual world, become a different version of who you are in real life, be it for better or worse.

>> **Simulation:** Rather than live in the virtual world of some game designer, create and manage your own virtual world.

>> **Sports:** Electronic interpretations of real-world activities that incorporate some of the skill or strategy elements of the original game; vary based upon the level of detail.

>> **Strategy:** Emphasize decision-making skills, like chess; a variety of games with varying levels of complexity and agreement with reality.

>> **Trivia:** A variety of games that reward you if you know things like the name of the family dog from the TV show *My Three Sons.* Its name was Tramp, but you knew that already.

>> **Word:** Games that are universally popular, such as Scrabble.

TIP

Many games appear in more than one category.

Each game has a Description page. It's similar to the Description page for apps, but it emphasizes different attributes. Figure 10-5 is an example Description page.

FIGURE 10-5:
A Description page for Flow Free.

When you're in a category that looks promising, look for these road signs to help you check out and narrow your choices among similar titles:

>> **Ratings/Comments:** Gamers love to exalt good games and bash bad ones. The comments for the game shown in Figure 10-5 are complimentary, and the overall ranking next to the game name at the top suggests that many others are favorable.

>> **Description:** This tells you the basic idea behind the game.

>> **What's New:** This section tells what capabilities have been added since the previous release. This is relevant if you have an earlier version of this game.

- » **Reviews:** Here is where existing users get to vent their spleen if they do not like the game or brag about how smart they are for buying it ahead of you. The comments are anonymous, include the date the comment was left, and tell you the kind of device the commenter used. There can be applications that lag on some older devices. However, you have the Galaxy S8, which has the best of everything (for now).

- » **More Games by Developer:** If you have a positive experience with a given game, you may want to check that developer's other games. The More By section makes it easier for you to find these other titles.

- » **Users Also Viewed/Users Also Installed:** This shows you the other apps that other people who downloaded this app have viewed or downloaded. These are some apps that you may want to check out.

- » **Price:** As a tie-breaker among similar titles, a slightly higher price is a final indication of a superior game. And because you're only talking a few pennies, price isn't usually a big deal.

Leaving Feedback on Games

For applications in general, and games in particular, the Play Store is a free market. When you come in to the Play Store, your best path to finding a good purchase is to read the reviews of those who have gone before you. Although more than a million users have commented on Angry Birds, most games do not have that kind of following.

One could argue that your opinion would not move the overall rating for a frequently reviewed game like Angry Birds. The same cannot be said for other games.

One of the new paid games is Dungeoneers from Monsterious Games. The game description is shown in Figure 10-6.

REMEMBER

A Description page, before you download it to your phone, will show either the Install button or the price of the game; the feedback areas will be grayed out. The Description page after you download the game to your phone will offer the options to Open or Uninstall, and the feedback areas will be active.

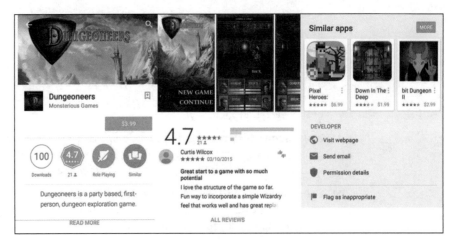

FIGURE 10-6:
A game
description for
Dungeoneers.

In this case, Dungeoneers has been reviewed by 21 gamers, most of whom are pretty darn enthusiastic. Your opinion matters more for this game than for the heavily reviewed games. After you've downloaded and played a game, you can help make the system work by providing your own review. This section reviews the process, starting from the first screen of the Play Store, which was shown in Figure 10-1:

1. **Tap the Menu icon.**

   This brings up a pop-up menu like the one shown in Figure 10-7.

2. **Tap My Apps.**

   This brings up the applications that you've downloaded, as shown in Figure 10-8. The Play Store does not distinguish between games and apps. They're all in the same list.

3. **Tap the game for which you'd like to leave feedback.**

   Tapping the title of the game normally brings up the game description similar to what is shown in Figures 10-5 and 10-6. After you've downloaded a game, however, a Rate & Review section appears that lets you leave feedback. See Figure 10-9 to see this section for Angry Birds.

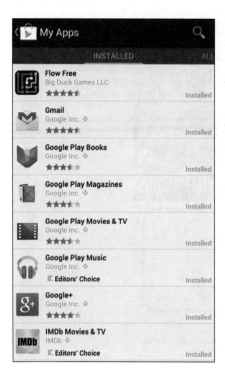

FIGURE 10-7:
The pop-up
menu for the
Play Store
applications.

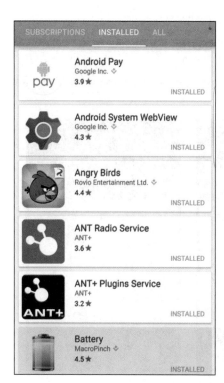

FIGURE 10-8:
Check out your
downloads.

FIGURE 10-9:
The Game
Description
page with
space for feed-
back.

Review section

4. **Tap the stars on the screen.**

    This brings up a pop-up screen, as shown on the left of Figure 10-10.

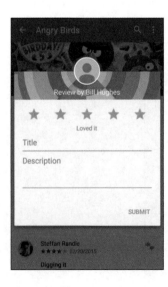 

FIGURE 10-10:
The ratings
stars pop-up
screen before
and after
entering feed-
back.

5. **Tap the number of stars you believe this game deserves.**

The right image shown in Figure 10-10 illustrates the result for a five-star review.

You then make a name for your review and enter any comments. You cannot enter comments without first choosing the number of stars for this game.

6. **When you're done, tap Submit.**

Your comments are sent to the Play Store for everyone to see. For the sake of the system, make sure your comments are accurate!

Chapter **11**

Mapping Out Where You Want to Be

H aving a map on your phone is a very handy tool. At the most basic level, you can ask your phone to show you a map for where you plan to go. This is convenient, but only a small part of what you can do.

With the right applications, your Galaxy S8 phone can do the following:

» Automatically find your location on a map

» Give directions to where you want to go

- As you drive, using historical driving times

- As you drive, using real-time road conditions

- While you walk

- As you take public transportation

» Give turn-by-turn directions as you travel

- With two-dimensional representations of the road and intersections

- With three-dimensional representations of the roads, buildings, and intersections

>> Tell others where you are

>> Use the screen on your phone as a viewfinder to identify landmarks as you pan the area (augmented reality)

There are also some mapping applications for the Galaxy S8 for commercial users, such as MyBusVue from Zonar Systems or Live Truck Tracking from Real Green Systems, but I don't cover them in this book.

GPS 101: First Things First

You can't talk smartphone mapping without GPS in the background, which creates a few inherent challenges of which you need to be aware. First off (and obviously), there is a GPS receiver in your phone. That means the following:

>> **Gimme a sec.** Like all GPS receivers, your location-detection system takes a little time to determine your location when you first turn on your phone.

>> **Outdoors is better.** Many common places where you use your phone — primarily, within buildings — have poor GPS coverage.

>> **Nothing is perfect.** Even with good GPS coverage, location and mapping aren't perfected yet. *Augmented reality,* the option that identifies local landmarks on the screen, is even less perfect. More about that in Chapter 14.

>> **You must be putting me on.** Your GPS receiver must be turned on for it to work. Sure, turning it off saves battery life, but doing so precludes mapping applications from working.

>> **Keep it on the down-low.** Sharing sensitive location information is of grave concern to privacy advocates. The fear is that a stalker or other villain can access your location information in your phone to track your movements. In practice, there are easier ways to accomplish this goal, but controlling who knows your location is still something you should consider, particularly when you have applications that share your location information.

REMEMBER

Good cellular coverage has nothing to do with GPS coverage. The GPS receiver in your phone is looking for satellites; cellular coverage is based upon antennas mounted on towers or tall buildings.

TIP

Mapping apps are useful, but they also use more battery life and data than many other applications. Be aware of the impact on your data usage and battery life. Leaving mapping applications active is convenient, but it can also be a drain on your battery and your wallet if you don't pay attention to your usage and have the wrong service plan.

Practically Speaking: Using Maps

The kind of mapping application that's easiest to understand is one that presents a local map when you open the application. Depending on the model of your phone, you may have a mapping applications preloaded, such as Google Maps, TeleNav, or VZ Navigator. You can find them on your Home screen and in your Application list.

It's not a large leap for a smartphone to offer directions from your GPS-derived location to somewhere you want to go in the local area. These are standard capabilities found in each of these applications.

REMEMBER

This section describes Google Maps and Google Maps Navigation; these are both free and may come preinstalled on your phone. If not, you can download them from the Google Play Store. Other mapping applications that may come with your phone, such as Bing Maps or TeleNav, have similar capabilities, but the details will be a bit different. Or you may want to use other mapping applications. That's all fine.

In addition to the general-purpose mapping applications that come on your phone, hundreds of available mapping applications can help you find a favorite store, navigate waterways, or find your car in a crowded parking lot. For example, Navigon and Waze offer solutions that base their navigation on real-time traffic conditions and give you turn-by-turn directions using three-dimensional images of the neighborhoods in which you are driving. For more, see the section, "Upgrading Your Navigation," at the end of this chapter.

WARNING

As nice as mapping devices are, they're too slow to tell you to stop looking at them and avoid an oncoming car. If you can't control yourself in the car and need to watch the arrow on the map screen move, do yourself a favor and let someone else drive. If no one else is available to drive, be safe and don't use the navigation service on your phone in the car.

The most basic way to use a map is to bring up the Google Maps application. The icon for launching this app is shown here.

The first screen that you see when you tap the Google Maps icon is a street map with your location. Figure 11-1 shows an example of a map when the phone user is in the Seattle area.

The location of the user is a blue arrow head at the center of the map. The resolution of the map in the figure starts at about one square mile. You can see other parts of the map by placing a finger on the map and dragging away from the part of the map that you want to see. That brings new sections of the map onto the screen.

Map Menu   Search Box   Voice Commands

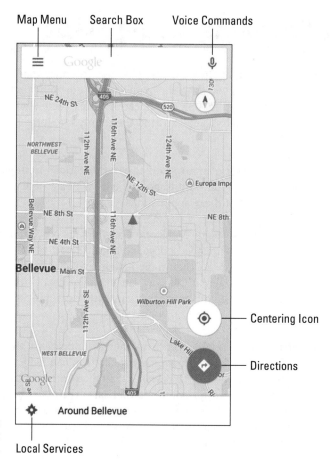

Centering Icon

Directions

FIGURE 11-1:
You start
where you are.

Local Services

Turn the phone to change how the map is displayed. Depending on what you're looking for, a different orientation might be easier.

TIP

Changing map scale

A resolution of one square mile will work, under some circumstances, to help you get oriented in an unfamiliar place. But sometimes it helps to zoom out to get a broader perspective or zoom in to find familiar landmarks, like a body of water or a major highway.

To get more real estate onto the screen, use the pinch motion I discuss in Chapter 2. This shrinks the size of the map and brings in more of the map around where you're pinching. If you need more real estate on the screen, you can keep pinching until you get more and more map. After you have your bearings, you can return to the original resolution by double-tapping the screen.

On the other hand, a scale of one square mile may not be enough. To see more landmarks, use the stretch motion to zoom in. The stretch motion expands the boundaries of the place where you start the screen. Continue stretching and stretching until you get the detail that you want. Figure 11-2 shows a street map both zoomed in and zoomed out. The map on the left is zoomed in in Satellite view. The map on the right is zoomed out in Terrain view.

Zoomed In Image

Panned Out Image

FIGURE 11-2:
A street image zoomed in and zoomed out.

The app gives you the choice of Satellite view or Terrain view by tapping the menu button, the three parallel lines, on the top-left corner of the map. This brings up a pop-up menu similar to the one shown in Figure 11-3.

Bring up the Satellite view by tapping Satellite. You get the Terrain view by tapping Terrain. You can also bring up other views that are useful to you, including transit routes and bicycling paths. I show you some of the other options in the next section in this chapter.

TIP

If you're zooming in and can't find where you are on the map, tap the dot-surrounded-by-a-circle icon (refer to Figure 11-1 for the centering icon). It moves the map so that you're in the center.

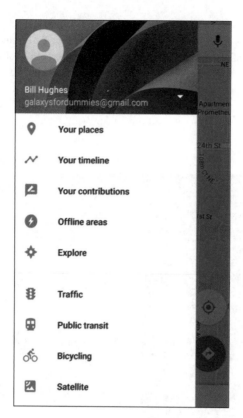

FIGURE 11-3:
The Map menu
pop-up.

Finding nearby services

Most searches for services fall into a relatively few categories. Your Maps application is set up to find what you're most likely to seek. By tapping the Local Services icon at the bottom of the page (refer to Figure 11-1), you're offered a quick way to find the services near you, such as restaurants, coffee shops, bars, hotels, attractions, ATMs, and gas stations, as shown in Figure 11-4.

Not only that, it is aware of the time of day. There are different suggestions during breakfast time than in the evening. Just scroll down and tap one of the topical icons, and your phone performs a search of businesses in your immediate area. The results come back as a regular Google search with names, addresses, and distances from your location. An example is shown in Figure 11-5.

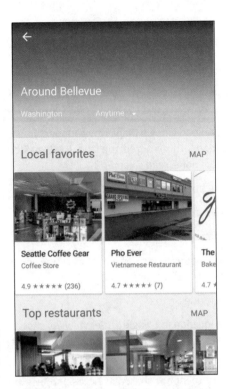

FIGURE 11-4:
Tap to find
a service on
the map.

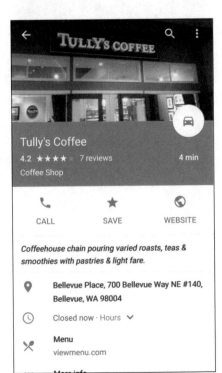

FIGURE 11-5:
The results
of a service
selection.

In addition to the location and reviews, the search results include icons and other relevant information:

TIP

>> **Directions:** Tap the car icon to get turn-by-turn directions from your location to this business.

You might need to download Google Maps Navigation to your phone to get the turn-by-turn directions. This is a free app from the Play Store. For more on how to download applications, read Chapter 8.

>> **Call:** Tap this to call the business.

>> **Save:** Tap the star to set this place as one of your favorites.

>> **Website:** Tap this to be taken to the website for this business.

>> **Map:** Tap the Google location icon to see a map of where you are in relation to this business, but without directions.

>> More options, which include

- *Street View:* See the location in Google Street View. As shown at the bottom of Figure 11-6, Street View shows a photo of the street address for the location you entered.

- *Hours:* If this establishment has shared its hours of operation, you can find them here.

- *Menu:* If this establishment has shared its menu, you can find it here.

- *Reviews:* This includes all kinds of information about what people have experienced this location.

- *More:* Run another Google search on this business to get additional information, such as reviews from other parts of the web.

Just how deeply you dive into using this information is up to you. In any case, having this kind of information when you're visiting an unfamiliar location is handy.

FIGURE 11-6:
A street map
search result.

Getting and Using Directions

You probably want to get directions from your map application. I know I do. You can get directions in a number of ways, including

» Tap the Search text box and enter the name or address of your location — for example, Seattle Space Needle or 742 Evergreen Terrace, Springfield, IL.

» Tap the Services icons (refer to Figure 11-2), tap the Attractions icon (refer to Figure 11-4), and select your location.

Any of these methods lead you to the map showing your location, as shown in Figure 11-6.

It might seem intuitive to expect that when you search for a specific attraction (such as the Seattle Space Needle), you get only the Seattle Space Needle. Such a result, however, is sometimes too simple. A given search may have multiple results, such as for chain stores. Google Map gives you several choices, and you may need to choose your favorite. Typically, the app will give you the closest option.

To get directions, tap the Directions icon. This brings up the pop-up screen shown in Figure 11-7.

FIGURE 11-7:
Your direction
options, from
original location
to the target.

This gives you the options of

>> **Driving:** Turn-by-turn directions as you drive from where you are to the destination.

>> **Public Transportation:** This option tells you how to get to your destination by taking public transportation using published schedules.

>> **Cycling:** This option is for the cyclists among us; it includes bike trails in addition to city streets.

>> **Walking Navigation:** Turn-by-turn directions as you walk to your destination.

For each of these options, you can use the options at the bottom of the screen to

» **Get Directions:** Sequential directions, as shown in Figure 11-8, but without telling you when to turn.

» **Navigate:** Rather than show you a map, this option puts you in a navigation app that monitors where you are as you travel and tells you what to do next.

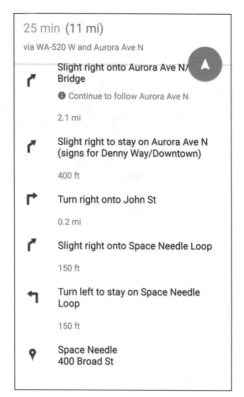

FIGURE 11-8: Step-by-step directions to the target.

Upgrading Your Navigation

As a rule, free navigation applications like Google Maps Navigation use historical averages to determine travel times. The applications that charge a modest monthly fee (between $5 and $10 monthly), like VZ Navigator, have real-time updates that avoid taking you on congested routes. They also tend to have 3D images that provide better context for landmarks. (See Figure 11-9.)

2D Navigation

3D Navigation

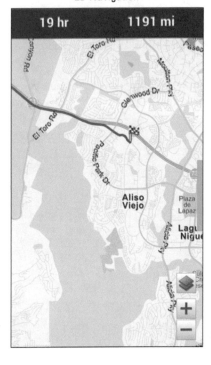

FIGURE 11-9:
Comparing 2D
navigation to
3D navigation.

As you can see in Figure 11-9, the 2D map is perfectly usable and accurate, but the 3D map gives you context and additional information about the buildings around you, which can give you an extra level of confidence. So if you frequently depend on your mapping app to get where you're going, you may find it worth your while to spend money for a paid app.

REMEMBER

Paying an extra $5 to $10 monthly feels like a lot for some of us. Keep in mind, however, that

>> This amount is relatively modest compared to what you're paying monthly for your service.

>> The price of a dedicated GPS receiver, with almost exactly the same capabilities, is between $125 and $200. The monthly cost of the service is comparable to the one-time fee of the GPS receiver. Plus, you don't have the hassle of lugging an additional device and its wiring.

TIP

Sometimes the app gives audio instructions. The Google App has a speaker icon that appears on the map that allows you to turn audio instructions on or off.

DRIVING SAFELY

Using your phone while driving is a bad idea. Texting while driving is illegal in most states, but studies have shown that laws don't affect behavior that much. It's just so darn tempting to sneak a peek at your phone. The grim reality: According to the National Highway Transportation Administration, texting while driving resulted in more than 600 deaths in the United States in 2014. When you include all the sources of distracted driving (eating, drinking, adjusting the radio, and so on), 3,179 people were killed and 431,000 were injured in 1.3 million accidents.

To make matters worse, distracted driving is disproportionately problematic for younger drivers. You can't do much to stop your teen from checking out his hair in the rearview mirror while he's driving, but you can install an app on his phone that will prevent him from texting while the car is in motion. The simplest apps track speed — if the phone is going above some preset limit, it shuts off the phone's communication. More sophisticated apps give you more options, including the ability to place calls to 911 or a list of exceptions, a code that you can enter if you're the passenger and not the driver, and more.

If you have trouble setting down your phone, you may even want to install one of these apps for yourself *and* for your teen.

IN THIS CHAPTER

» **Enjoying a single song, podcasts, or an entire album**

» **Viewing videos**

» **Knowing your licensing options**

Chapter **12**

Playing Music and Videos

S martphones have built-in digital music and video players. Some people hesitate to give up on their MP3 or portable multimedia players. This is simply technological inertia.

Having a single device that you can use as a phone *and* as a source of music is quite convenient because then you need only one device rather than two, and you eliminate extra cords for charging and separate headphones for listening. Your Samsung Galaxy S8 is no exception. You can play digital music files and podcasts all day and all night on your phone.

In addition, by virtue of the Super AMOLED screen on your Galaxy S8 smartphone, your phone makes for an excellent handheld video player. Just listen on the headset and watch on the screen, whether you have a short music video or a full-length movie.

To boot, your Galaxy S8 comes with applications for downloading and listening to music as well as downloading and watching videos. These apps are very straightforward, especially if you've ever used a CD or a DVD player. I will judge the success of this chapter by the number of MP3 and CD players that readers list on eBay.

Being Mindful of Carrier Quirks

The only possible pitfall for playing music and videos on your smartphone is that each cellular carrier has its own spin: Some carriers want you to use their proprietary music stores; some give you the freedom to enjoy the flexibility that comes with owning an Android-based phone. You can use the basic multimedia tools that come with the phone or download the myriad options that you have via the Play Store. (Read all about the Play Store in Chapter 8.)

To keep things straight, read on to see the options you have regardless of what cellular carrier you use — including the use of the basic multimedia applications that came with your phone. Lots and lots of options for entertainment exist out there. The truth is that there isn't that much difference among them when it comes to playing. The differences lie in price and selection.

Therefore, I cover the basic functions, but I encourage you to find the entertainment that you prefer. Trust me — it's out there somewhere. Find the music you like and subscribe to as many services as it takes to bring you joy. Remember, the whole point is enjoyment. Enjoy yourself!

Getting Ready to Be Entertained

Regardless of the model phone you have, the particular app you use for entertainment, and whether you're listening to audio or watching video, here's where I cover some common considerations up front.

The first is the use of headsets. Yeah, you use *headphones* with your MP3 player, but you probably want to use a *headset* with your phone. The vocabulary is more than just semantics; a headset has headphones plus a microphone on the cable. This makes it easier for when you get a call while listening to music or watching a movie.

Your phone sees an incoming call and will pause the music or movie and show you the caller ID. If you answer it and you have a headset, you can be reasonably assured that the person on the other line will hear you loud and clear. If you have headphones, the phone will use the built-in microphone for your voice while you hear the caller on your headphones. My advice is to test the sound quality using a headphone and judge for yourself whether you want to use a headset or headphones.

Next, I explore speakers. I touch on speakers in Chapters 3 when talking about Bluetooth pairing and again in Chapter 16 when I talk about making the phone your own. As you may guess, having a solid strategy for speakers is important to get the most out of your Galaxy S8.

Then you need to know about connecting your Galaxy S8 phone to a television and/or stereo. After I talk about that, I cover the issue of licensing multimedia material.

Finally, I explore storing all these options on your phone for your offline enjoyment. You can have gobs of storage at your disposal if you want. I explore what the term "gobs" really means in terms of audio and video storage.

Choosing your headset

You can use wired or wireless (Bluetooth) headsets with your Samsung Galaxy S8 phone. Wired headsets are less expensive than Bluetooth headsets, and, of course, wired headsets don't need charging, as do the Bluetooth headsets.

On the other hand, you lose freedom of mobility if you're tangled up in wires. In addition, the battery in Bluetooth headsets lasts much longer than the battery in your phone.

Wired headsets

At the bottom of your Galaxy S8 phone is a headset jack. If you try to use your regular headphone jack in this jack, you'll hear the audio, but the person on the other end of the call may not hear you because the headphones don't come with a microphone. In such a case, your phone tries to use the built-in mic as a speakerphone. Depending upon the ambient noise conditions, it may work fine or sound awful. Of course, you can always ask the person you're talking to whether he or she can hear you.

To address that problem, your phone might come with a wired headset. In that case, just plug it in to use the device. The Galaxy S8 uses ear buds, like those shown in Figure 12-1.

Some people dislike ear buds. You can obtain other styles at a number of retail franchises that offer options, including

>> Around-the-ear headphones that place the speakers on the ear and are held in place with a clip

>> A behind-the-neck band that holds around-the-ear headphones in place

>> An over-the-head band that places the headphones on the ear

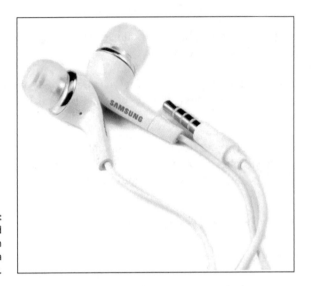

FIGURE 12-1:
A typical wired
headset with
ear buds and a
3.5mm plug.

WARNING

The laws in some regions prohibit the use of headphones while driving. Correcting the officer and explaining that these are really "headsets" and not "headphones" won't help your case if you're pulled over. Even if not explicitly illegal in an area, it's still a bad idea to play music in both ears at a volume that inhibits your ability to hear warnings while driving.

WARNING

Ear buds can have a greater chance of causing ear damage if the volume is too loud than other options. The close proximity to your eardrum is the culprit. There are probably warnings on the ear bud instructions, but I wanted to amplify this information (<har har>).

In any case, give yourself some time to get used to any new headset. There is often an adjustment period while you get used to having a foreign object in or around your ear.

Stereo Bluetooth headsets

The other option is to use a stereo Bluetooth headset. Figure 12-2 shows a few options.

You need to consider a few important options before you put down your money and buy one. First, you have a choice of the earpieces being "on" the ear, "over" the ear, or "in" the ear.

Over-the-ear
headset

In-the-ear headset

On-the-ear
headphone

FIGURE 12-2:
Bluetooth
stereo
headsets.

The over-the-ear option tends to eliminate outside noise a little better because your ears are surrounded by the cushions. This can also get hot if you wear your headphones for an extended time. Figure 12-2 shows the Plantronics Backbeat Pro. This headset has the added capability of connecting to two Bluetooth devices at the same time. It has the smarts to jump between these devices. For example, I may be watching a course delivered on my laptop. When a call comes in on my cellphone, this headset will pause the video and allow me to take the call. How slick is that?

The on-the-ear headphone is good for when you have your headphones on for a long time. The on-the-ear headphone seen in Figure 12-2 is a Bedphone that is designed specifically for use in bed, including as you sleep. How cool is that?

The third option for headsets includes those that insert into your ear canal. These ear buds are just wires and plugs and have some structure to stay on your head. Having this kind of headset in your ear makes it less likely to shift or fall out than the other options. The in-the-ear headset shown in Figure 12-2 is well-suited for those who want to listen to music and have the ability to take calls has they exercise. How neat is that?

In each of these cases, a stereo Bluetooth headset is paired the same way as any other Bluetooth headset. (Read how to do this in Chapter 3.) When your Galaxy S8 phone and the headset connect, the phone recognizes that the headset operates in stereo when you're listening to music or videos.

Choosing your Bluetooth speaker

In the last few years, developers released a flurry of products known as *Bluetooth speakers.* Among the better-known Bluetooth speakers are products, such as the Dre Beats Pill. These speakers include a range of options, some of which are a very small and convenient. Others are designed to offer excellent audio quality.

Although these speakers (which come in a range of sizes) are not as portable as the Bluetooth headset — they're a little difficult to use as you're walking down the street — they're usually pretty easy to take with you and set up when you're at a desk or in someone's living room. They also do not need a cable to make a connection and are always ready to go.

Soen Audio's Transit (see Figure 12-3) is an excellent example of a high-quality Bluetooth speaker. Its list price is close to $200.

FIGURE 12-3:
The Soen
Audio Transit
Bluetooth
speaker.

If you like high-quality sound, this is the quality of Bluetooth speaker that you'd want to get. On the other hand, if you're just looking for background enjoyment, you can get a Bluetooth speaker for less than half that price.

Connecting to your stereo

Although being able to listen to your music on the move is convenient, it's also nice to be able to listen to your music collection on your home or car stereo. Your Galaxy S8 phone presents your stereo with a nearly perfect version of what went in. The sound quality that comes out is limited only by the quality of your stereo.

In addition, you can play the music files and playlists stored on your phone, which can be more convenient than playing CDs. If your stereo receiver is older, setup involves plugging the 3.5mm jack from the cable shown in Figure 12-4 into the 3.5mm jack available on newer stereos.

FIGURE 12-4:
The patch
cable with
3.5mm plugs.

When you play the music as you do through a headset, it will play through your stereo. Although each stereo system is unique, the correct setting for the selector knob is AUX.

Newer stereo receivers recognize that cellular phones are a great place to access music. These receivers support a Bluetooth connection to your phone. If you are in the market for a new receiver, make sure that you get one with Bluetooth capability. In either case, you will be entertained. Enjoy yourself.

Licensing Your Multimedia Files

It's really quite simple: You need to pay the artist if you're going to listen to music or watch video with integrity. Many low-cost options are suitable for any budget. Depending upon how much you plan to listen to music or podcasts, or watch videos, you can figure out what's the best deal.

WARNING

Stealing music or videos is uncool. Although it might be technically possible to play pirated music and videos on your phone, it's stealing. Don't do it. If your financial circumstances do not allow you to afford to pay for your music, I suggest you listen to Internet Radio. With just a little work on your part, you can get free unlimited music and at least a low monthly fee if you want no advertising.

You can buy or lease music, podcasts, or videos. In most cases, you pay for them with a credit card. And depending upon your cellular carrier, you might be allowed to pay for them on your monthly cellular bill.

Listening up on licensing

Here are the three primary licensing options available for music files and podcasts:

>> **By the track:** Pay for each song individually. Buying a typical song costs about 79 cents to $1.29. Podcasts, which are frequently used for speeches or lectures, can vary dramatically in price.

>> **By the album:** Buying an album isn't a holdover from the days before digital music. Music artists and producers create albums with an organization of songs that offer a consistent feeling or mood. Although many music-playing applications allow you to assemble your own playlist, an album is created by professionals. In addition, buying a full album is often less expensive than on a per-song basis. You can get multiple songs for $8 to $12.

>> **With a monthly pass:** The last option for buying audio files is the monthly pass. For about $15 per month, you can download as much music as you want from the library of the service provider.

TECHNICAL STUFF

If you let your subscription to your monthly pass provider lapse, you won't be able to listen to the music from this library. This music is *streamed* through the Internet and not stored on your phone.

In addition to full access to the music library, some music library providers offer special services to introduce you to music that's similar to what you've been playing. These services are a very convenient way to learn about new music. If you have even a small interest in expanding your music repertoire, these services are an easy way to do it.

Whether buying or renting is most economical depends on your listening/viewing habits. If you don't plan to buy much, or you know specifically what you want, you may save some money by paying for all your files individually. If you're not really sure what you want, or you like a huge variety of music, paying for monthly access might make better sense for you.

Licensing for videos

The two primary licensing options available for videos are

>> **Rental:** This option is similar to renting a video from a store. You can view the video as many times as you like within 24 hours from the start of the first play. In addition, the first play must begin within a defined period, such as a week, of your downloading it. Most movies are in the $3 to $5 range.

>> **Purchase:** You have a license to view the file as frequently as you want, for as long as you want. The purchase cost can be as low as $12, but is more typically in the $15 range.

At the moment, there are no sources for mainstream Hollywood films that allow you to buy a monthly subscription and give you unlimited access to a film library. This can change at any time, so watch for announcements.

Using the Full Capacity of Your SD Card

Your Galaxy S8 comes with 64GB of storage. Okay. What does that really mean?

The Android operating system is stored on some of that storage space. Plus, the apps that you downloaded are stored here. Then, there are the files that you create and use. After it is all said and done, you probably have at least 30GB available for the storage of photos, music, and videos. So how much is that, and do you need more?

The correct answer is, "Who knows?" That is about as worthless of an answer as you will find anywhere in this book. However, I can tell you how to change that response to "It doesn't matter."

Your phone has a slot in the top where you can add a microSD card, and your Android operating system can address an additional 256GB of storage. Okay. So how much is that?

The easiest way to describe it is by figuring out how many photos, how many songs, and how many movies fit into 1GB.

>> **300 images:** You can take about 300 images from the camera on your phone at resolution at the default settings.

>> **Ten hours of music:** If you buy an album, it will take somewhat less than a tenth of a gigabyte. The length of albums was set based upon what could be reliably imprinted on a vinyl record. That works out to be about 45 minutes and maybe a dozen songs.

>> **About one standard definition (TV-quality) movie:** Estimating the size of videos can get really variable. TV quality video is a waste of that beautiful screen. However, an hour of video that uses every pixel of resolution will take about 4GB.

Unfortunately, at this point, you need to do a little bit of math. Say that I want to watch every minute of all 529 episodes of *The Simpsons*. This would take 194 hours or about 8 days. All I need to do is buy a 200GB chip for about $80, load it up, and put it in my phone. D'oh!

You could binge-watch all the episodes of the series *Breaking Bad* in high definition on one SD card. If you want to be able to binge-watch *Breaking Bad* and *The Walking Dead*, it would need to be stored in standard mode. Sorry.

If you are more into music than videos, you could store over 2,500 music albums on that poor microSD Card. The albums could include *Ella Fitzgerald Sings the Gershwin Songbook* and *Chicago at Carnegie Hall,* each of which is well over three hours.

Keep in mind that these are rough estimates. These calculations assume there are minor attempts to reduce the size of these files. That can have a huge impact on storage needs. Let's just say that you can put a combination of images, music, and video that will keep you entertained for a very, very long time.

Enjoying Basic Multimedia Capabilities

Regardless of the version of your Galaxy S8, some basic multimedia capabilities are common across the different phones. Figure 12-5 shows the Music and Video applications.

FIGURE 12-5:
The multimedia apps on the Galaxy S8.

Your phone comes with these applications preloaded, and you might have other multimedia applications as well, depending upon your carrier.

Grooving with the Play Music app

The Play Music app allows you to play music and audio files. The first step is to obtain music and audio files for your phone.

Some ways to acquire music and/or recordings for your phone are

» Buy and download tracks from an online music store.

» Receive them as attachments via email or text message.

» Receive them from another device connected with a Bluetooth link.

» Record them on your phone.

Buying from an online music store

The most straightforward method of getting music on your phone is from an online music store. You can download a wide variety of music from dozens of mainstream online music stores. The Play Store is an option. In addition to apps, it has music and video. Other well-known sites include Rhapsody, Amazon Music, and last.fm.

In addition, many more specialty or "boutique" stores provide more differentiated offerings than you can get from the mass-market stores. For example, MAQAM offers Middle Eastern music (www.maqammp3.com).

The details for acquiring music among the online stores vary from store to store. Ultimately, there are more similarities than differences. As an example of when you know what you want, what you really, really want, here's how to find and download the song "Wannabe" by the Spice Girls. I'm using Amazon Music. If you don't have Amazon Music in your Applications list, you would start by loading that app on your phone, as I describe how to do in Chapter 8. After entering your Amazon sign-in information, you see the Amazon Music Home screen, shown on the right in Figure 12-6.

Amazon MP3 sign-in screen

Amazon MP3 Music Store Home screen

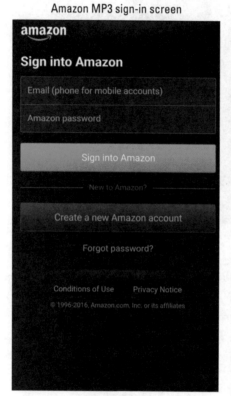
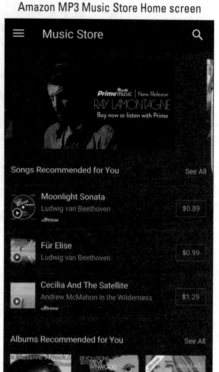

FIGURE 12-6: The Amazon Music login and Home screens.

From here, you can search for music by album, song, or music genre. Now to search for the song you want:

1. **Enter the relevant search information in the Amazon Music Search field.**

   In this case, I'm searching for "Wannabe" by the Spice Girls. The result of the search for songs looks like Figure 12-7.

FIGURE 12-7:
Search results
for a song at
the Amazon
Music store.

The search results come up with all kinds of options, including: albums, individual tracks, similar songs, karaoke versions, and other songs from the same artist. Be ready for these options.

2. **To purchase the track, tap twice on the price.**

The left screen in Figure 12-8 shows the price. When you tap once on the price, you get a confirmation message to make sure that you want to buy the download; the price is replaced with a Buy Song icon, as shown on the right in Figure 12-8. To buy, tap Buy Song.

3. **Expect to pay.**

Unless you're going to subsist on the free promotional songs, you need to pay. In this case, you get the screen shown in Figure 12-9.

The song is now loaded on your phone. When you open the music player, it's ready for you to play anytime you want to party like it's 1996!

Step 1

Step 2

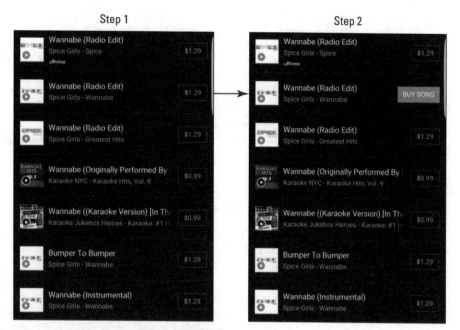

FIGURE 12-8:
Tap twice
to buy.

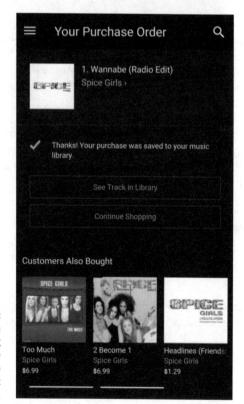

FIGURE 12-9:
The screen
confirming
your purchase
from the
Amazon Music
store.

Receiving music as an attachment

As long as you comply with your license agreement, you can email or text a music file as an attachment. Simply send yourself an email from your PC with the desired music file. You then open the email or text on your phone and save the file in the library of your Music app.

TECHNICAL STUFF

Your phone can play music files that come in any of the following formats: FLAC, WAV, Vorbis, MP3, AAC, AAC+, eAAC+, WMA, AMR-NB, AMR-WB, MID, AC3, and XMF.

Recording sounds on your phone

No one else might think your kids' rendition of "Happy Birthday" is anything special, but you probably treasure it. In fact, many sound recording apps are available on your phone.

Some are basic and turn your phone into a basic voice recorder. Others can alter your voice. (I do not want to know why.) Others are meant to allow you to surreptitiously record voice conversations. Some can specifically record telephone conversations.

TIP

Be aware of privacy laws in your area! Some jurisdictions require only one party in a conversation to give permission to record a conversation. Other jurisdictions require positive consent from all parties. While rare, there have been cases where first-time offenders have spent long stints in jail for recording what was perfectly legal in another state!

In general, a simple record button creates a sound file when you stop recording. The sound quality may not be the best, but what you record can be just as important or entertaining as what you buy commercially. Your phone treats all audio files the same and all are playable on your Play Music.

Playing downloaded music

Play Music

To play your music, tap the Play Music app icon (as shown in the margin) to open the music playing application.

Okay. Figure 12-10 shows your Home screen after your get through the initial marketing welcome. Sometimes this app can be too enthusiastic in welcoming you.

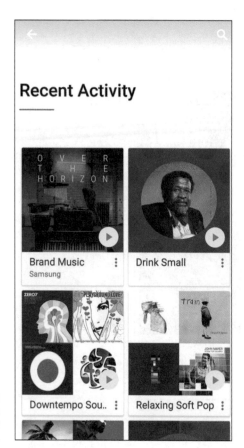

Recent Activity

Brand Music
Samsung

Drink Small

Downtempo Sou..

Relaxing Soft Pop

FIGURE 12-10:
Home screen
for the Play
Music app.

The first screen that you see sorts your music files into a number of categories. You can select the category you want to use by tapping on the link that says playlist. This brings up a pop-up screen.

The categories include

>> **Playlists:** Some digital music stores bundle songs into playlists, such as Top Hits from the '50s. You can also create your own playlists for groups of songs that are meaningful to you.

>> **Stations:** These are kind of like radio stations that follow a particular format. You put in a group name, like Genesis or Van Halen, and Play Music will play songs within that genre that may or may not be currently stored on your phone. Figure 12-11 shows a more recent example when I searched on Bruno Mars. The section later in this chapter on Internet Radio describes this service in more detail.

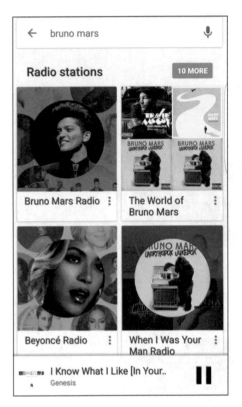

FIGURE 12-11:
Bruno Mars
Radio Station
within the Play
Music app.

>> **Artists:** This category lists all songs from all the albums from a given artist.

>> **Albums:** Tapping this category places all your songs into an album with which the song is associated. When you tap the album, you see all the songs you've purchased, whether one song or all the songs from that album.

>> **Songs:** This lists all your song files in alphabetic order.

>> **Genres:** This category separates music into music genres, such as country and western or heavy metal.

These categories are useful when you have a large number of files. To play a song, an album, or a genre, open that category and tap the song, playlist, album, artist, or genre, and the song will start playing.

Adding songs as ringtones and alarms

Here's how to add a song as a ringtone or alarm. The first step is to open a contact. A generic contact in Edit mode is seen in Figure 12-12. (Refer to Chapter 6 if you have any questions about contacts.)

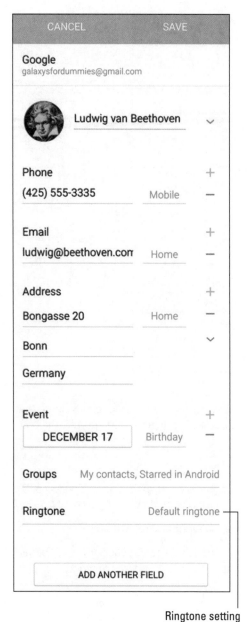

FIGURE 12-12:
A typical
contact for
a Baroque
composer.

Follow these steps:

1. **Tap the Default Ringtone link.**

   This will bring up a list of ringtones (shown in Figure 12-13).

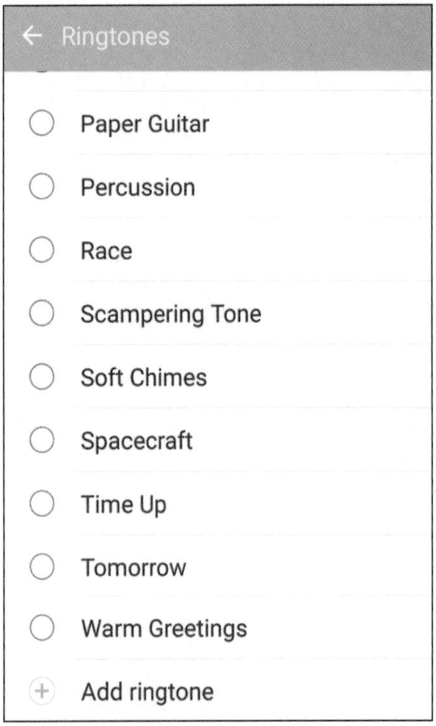

FIGURE 12-13:
Basic
ringtones.

A quick scan finds that *Ode to Joy* is not among the options that come with your phone. To use a music file as a ringtone, flick down to the bottom to find the Add button.

2. **Tap Add.**

   This brings up the option to bring up the Sound Picker App. This app shows all the music files on your phone, as shown in Figure 12-14.

3. **Highlight the song you want and tap OK.**

   From now on, when you hear this song, you know it will be your friend Ludwig. Figure 12-15 show that this is now Ludwig's ringtone.

Jamming to Internet Radio

If you have not tried Internet Radio, you should definitely consider it. The basic idea is that you enter information on your current music favorites, and these services play music that is similar. In some stations, a great deal of research with complex statistical analysis goes into picking similar songs based upon numeric analysis of musical patterns. Other stations wing it.

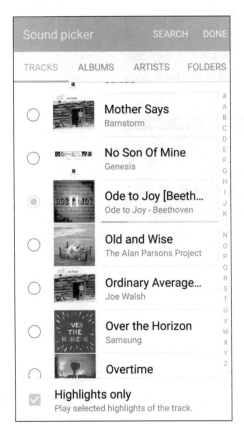

FIGURE 12-14:
The track
selections.

The good news is that you can explore your options. Figure 12-16 shows some of the 9,000 Internet Radio apps in the Play Store. Pandora and Slacker Radio are two of the best-known services of this type; one or the other may have been preinstalled on your phone. (Actually, you may find four or more Internet Radio options preinstalled on your phone!)

These apps are a great way to learn about new songs and groups that may appeal to you. The service streams music to your phone for you to enjoy. You can buy the track if you choose.

WARNING

Streaming audio files can use a large amount of data over time. This may be no problem if you have an unlimited (or even large) data-service plan. Otherwise, your "free" Internet Radio service can wind up costing you a lot. You're best off using Wi-Fi.

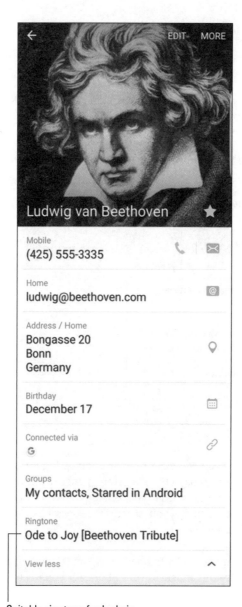

FIGURE 12-15:
FIGURE 12-15:
The ringtone
selection.

Suitable ringtone for Ludwig

The selection played by even the best Internet Radio can become repetitive after a while if you listen to it enough. If you find yourself bored, do not hesitate to switch Internet Radio providers and use the same band for the radio station. This will almost always bring up new songs.

TIP

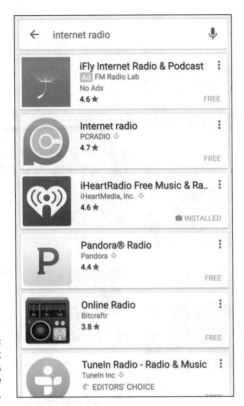

FIGURE 12-16:
Some Internet
Radio options
in the Play
Store.

Looking at your video options

The Play Music app allows you to play music files. Similarly, you use the Video Player app to play video options. The Video Player is in your Application list and might even be on your home page. In most ways, playing videos is the same as playing audio with some exceptions:

>> Many people prefer to buy music, but renting is more typical for videos.

>> Video files are usually, but not always, larger.

Otherwise, as with music files, you can acquire videos for your phone from an online video store — and you need to have an account and pay for the use. In addition, you can download video files to your phone, and the Video Player will play them like a DVD player.

There is a great selection of videos on the Google Play Store and Amazon Music. Each of these has great video selections that you can rent or buy. Figure 12-17 shows the Home screens for the Google Play Store and Amazon Video.

Play Store Video Home Page   Amazon Video Home Page

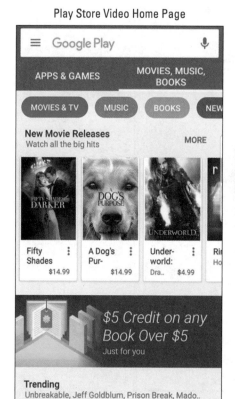

FIGURE 12-17:
Home screens
for Google
Play Store and
Amazon Video.

We should not forget Netflix, as seen in Figure 12-18.

Using the three screens

If you have a subscription to Netflix, I hereby grant you permission to watch any and all of the Netflix options on your Galaxy S8 (once you sign in and comply with all the terms and conditions set forth by Netflix). Once you install the Netflix app from the Play Store, sign in with the email and password associated with your account, and all the Netflix content is there for you to stream. It is that simple. If you don't believe me, give it a try.

If you take a look at the Netflix home page on the Internet, seen in Figure 12-19, it shows your options for access to the content to which you subscribe. The original term for this was called serving the *three screens.* Three screens referred to in the strategy included your television at home, your PC or laptop, and your smartphone.

FIGURE 12-18:
Getting Netflix
on your phone.

FIGURE 12-19:
The Netflix
home page.

The idea is that you get one subscription and have access to the same content and, importantly, can pick up where you left off. So if you're watching a video on your television, you can pick up where you left off on your smartphone.

Netflix is taking this one step further, as you can see in Figure 12-18, to ensure as many of its subscribers as possible have access. If you have a Smart TV that has an Internet connection, the chances are that Netflix will run on the TV. If you have an old and/or a dumb TV, you can get Netflix through streaming media players, game consoles, set-top boxes, or Blu-ray players.

Netflix is not the only organization to do this. Many cable companies offer this kind of solution, as do many of the video subscription services.

The mainstream video services compete with having a broad range within their libraries that seek to appeal to as many customers as possible. Keep in mind that there are specialty video providers that offer curated videos for their subscribers.

For example, TeacherTube is a site dedicated to K-12 education, as seen in Figure 12-20. If we continue down this path further, there are a great number of options for online education. Many of these sites do not consider themselves to be video aggregators, but that's exactly what happens when they take recorded lectures and provide them to students.

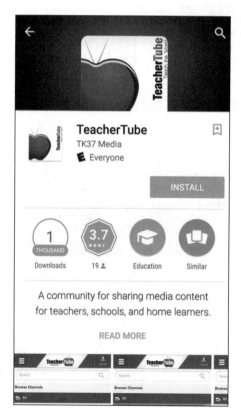

FIGURE 12-20:
The Teacher-
Tube app.

The best-known online education service is the University of Phoenix. There are dozens more online universities.

Education is just one curated video service. Others exist for videos of Bollywood movies, British sitcoms, Portuguese game shows, and many other art forms.

Viewing your own videos

In Chapter 9, I cover how to use the digital camcorder on your phone. You can watch any video you've shot on your phone. From the Google Play application, scroll over to the Personal Video section.

TECHNICAL
STUFF

Your phone can show the following video formats: MPEG-4, WMV, AVI/DivX, MKV, and FLV.

To play your video, simply tap the name of the file. The app begins showing the video in landscape orientation. The controls that pop up when you tap the screen are similar to the controls of a DVD player.

The reality of virtual reality

Video games can be immersive, and a good movie can really suck you into its reality. The idea of *virtual reality* is to take this one step further. The basic idea behind virtual reality is to create a simulated world by having you wear a pair of goggles and presenting images that change the screen based upon movements of your head and body.

We can explore the concept by taking it in steps. At the most basic level, you can use your phone with a pair of *virtual reality goggles.* Samsung is offering virtual reality goggles that are designed to work with your Galaxy S8. These are seen in Figure 12-21.

FIGURE 12-21:
Samsung virtual reality goggles.

What you do is insert your Galaxy S8 into the goggles. Then you use the little remote next to the goggles to navigate to the application. The remote is very convenient because, without it, the only way to communicate with the screen is by turning your head to commands and then holding it there for a few seconds. That little device allows you to navigate the screen while the phone is inserted in the goggles.

What happens is that your field of view is entirely taken up by the screen of your Galaxy S8. Imagine the most basic scenario, where the camera on the back of your phone shows you what is in front of you. This kind of experience is more or less comparable to using a pair of eyeglasses.

When you walk forward, things come closer. When you look down, you see the floor. When you turn your head to the right or the left, you see things that were not in your range of vision. So far, this is not very interesting.

So let's take it up a level. Now let's let your phone and all its processing capacity and intelligence tell you what you're looking at. You turn your head, and you see a picture. Presto chango, you see a little pop-up next to the picture that tells you that this is a print of Edward Hopper's *The Nighthawks.* You look out the window, and a pop-up appears with current weather conditions and a forecast for today.

Now you take your virtual reality goggles to the grocery store. As you get your cart, a familiar face comes up and starts talking. For the life of you, you cannot remember who this person is or how you know him. In just a moment, the face recognition system recognizes this person, and a pop-up identifies that this person is your old neighbor Bif Wellington. After chatting, you walk the store aisles looking for deals. You get a pop-up letting you know when this grocery is giving you a good deal on Honeycrisp apples, or if you can get them cheaper at the other store. This capability is called *augmented reality.*

Let's take it up another notch. Imagine a world where, instead of seeing a slightly modified version of your reality, you are transported to a beach. You can look around and see palm trees and jungles behind you.

Why stay earthbound? You are virtually transported to the space around Mars. As you look around, it is as if you are there on Mars.

Figure 12-22 looks like two images of the same planet. When your phone is inserted in the goggles, you get a 3-D image of the planet. You can also look around and navigate throughout the solar system. Trust me, this is a lot more convenient than space travel.

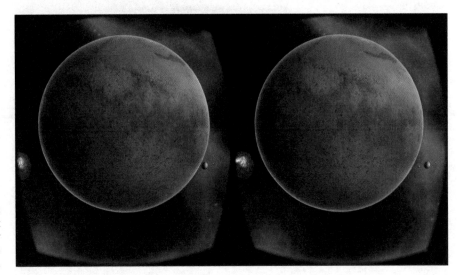

FIGURE 12-22:
A screen shot
from VR Solar
System from
Onepixelsoft.

Why stay in the mainstream opinion of what is reality? Now we can all have an "Alice through the Looking Glass" experience. You can grow and shrink and see all kinds of unusual visions which are limited by your imagination.

There are some very, very cool demonstrations that leverage the capabilities of your phone. The Samsung offering comes at a great price compared to some of the other options out there. For that matter, you may have received the Samsung virtual reality goggles for free for preordering your phone.

There are additional VR applications and content in the Play Store. This is a rapidly changing area of the Play Store where new content is constantly being added. Be sure to check the Play Store regularly.

This should make your friends who own iPhone technology suitably jealous. What needs to happen is further application development to really take us to where this technology can go.

WARNING

Some of us unfortunately have the unpleasant experience of what is called virtual-reality sickness. This is similar, but not identical, to seasickness and car sickness. The most common symptoms are nausea and headaches. If this happens to you, some of the medicines that help seasickness may help you avoid this unpleasant sensation. Some say it also helps to be seated when using virtual reality. Plus, symptoms tend to diminish over time as your brain gets used to this experience. If the symptoms are too severe, virtual reality may just not be for you.

5

Getting Down to Business

» **Downloading your calendars to your phone**

» **Uploading events to your PC**

Chapter **13**

Using the Calendar

You might fall in love with your Galaxy S8 phone so much that you want to ask it out on a date. And speaking of dates, let's talk about your phone's calendar. The Galaxy S8 phone calendar functions are powerful, and they can make your life easier. With just a few taps, you can bring all your electronic calendars together to keep your life synchronized.

In this chapter, I show you how to set up the calendar that comes with your phone, which might be all you need. The odds are, though, that you have calendars elsewhere, such as on your work computer. So I also show you how to combine all your calendars with your Galaxy S8 phone. After you read this chapter, you'll have no excuse for missing a meeting. (Or, okay, a date.)

TIP

Some calendars use the term *appointments* for *events*. They are the same idea. I use the term *events*.

Syncing Calendars

Most likely, you already have at least two electronic calendars scattered in different places: a calendar tied to your work computer and a personal calendar. Now you have a third one — the one on your Samsung phone that is synced to your Gmail account.

Bringing together all your electronic calendars to one place, though, is one of the best things about your phone — as long as you're a faithful user of your electronic calendars, that is. To begin this process, you need to provide authorization to the respective places that your calendars are stored in the same way as you authorized access to your email accounts and contacts in Chapters 5 and 6. This authorization is necessary to respect your privacy.

If your phone doesn't have a Calendar icon on the Home screen, open the Calendar app from your App list. This same app works with the calendar that's stored on your phone and any digital calendars that you add.

When you first open this app, you see a calendar in monthly format, as shown in Figure 13-1. I discuss other calendar views in the next section.

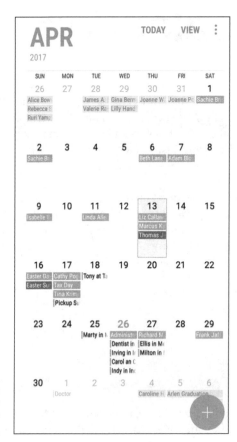

FIGURE 13-1: The monthly calendar display.

YOU MAY ALREADY BE A WINNER!

The calendar on your phone might already be populated with events from your work and personal calendars. Don't be concerned — this is good news!

If you've already set up your phone to *sync* (combine) with your email and your calendar (see Chapter 5), your calendars are already synchronizing with your phone.

When you add an account to your phone, such as your personal or work email account, your Facebook account, or Dropbox, you're asked whether you want to sync your calendar. The default setting for syncing is typically every hour.

Unless you get a warning message that alerts you to a communications problem, your phone now has the latest information on appointments and meeting requests. Your phone continues to sync automatically. It does all this syncing in the background; you may not even notice that changes are going on.

WARNING

You could encounter scheduling conflicts if others can create events for you on your digital calendar. Be aware of this possibility. It can be annoying (or worse) to think you have free time, offer it, and then find that someone else took it.

Setting Calendar Display Preferences

Before you get too far into playing around with your calendar, you'll want to choose how you view it.

If you don't have a lot of events, using the month calendar shown in Figure 13-1 is probably a fine option. On the other hand, if your day is jam-packed with personal and professional events, the daily or weekly schedules might prove more practical. Switching views is easy. For example, just tap the Month link at the top of the calendar, which in this case displays Apr 2016, to bring up the options. These are shown in Figure 13-2.

If you tap Week, you see the weekly display, as shown in Figure 13-3.

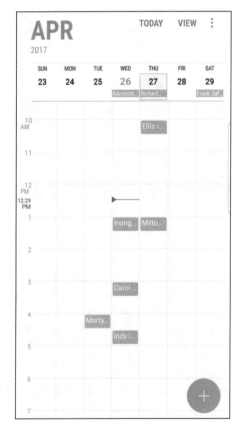

FIGURE 13-2:
The Calendar
Display Options
pop-up menu.

Year						
Month						
Week						
Day						
Tasks						

APR
2017

SUN	MON	TUE	WED	THU	FRI	SAT
23	24	25	26	27	28	29

FIGURE 13-3:
The weekly
calendar
display.

222   PART 5 Getting Down to Business

Or tap the Day button at the top of the calendar to show the daily display, as shown in Figure 13-4.

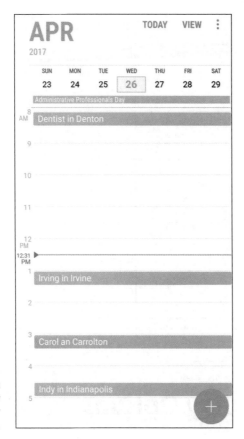

FIGURE 13-4:
The daily
calendar
display.

To see what events you have upcoming, regardless of the day they're on, you might prefer List view. Tap the List button at the top of the calendar to see a list of your activities.

TIP

The weekly and daily calendars show only a portion of the day. You can slide the screen to see the time slots earlier and later. You can also pinch and stretch to seem more or less of the time slots.

There is also an annual calendar, as seen in Figure 13-5. This is so busy that it does not allow you to see any appointments. It is primarily useful for setting dates out in the future.

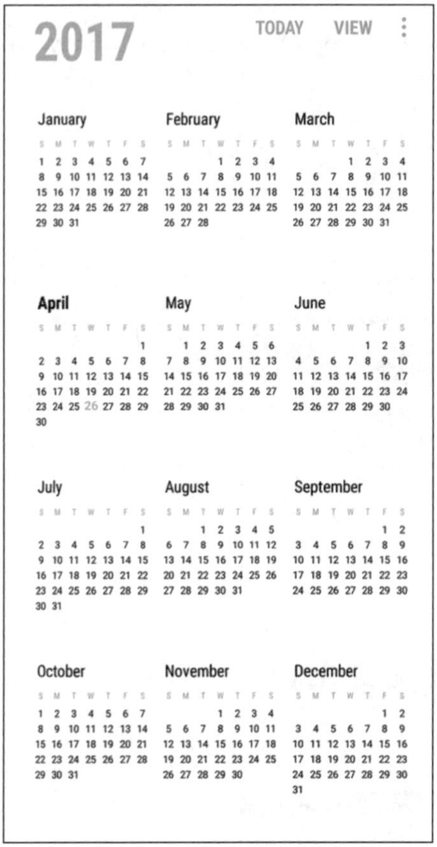

FIGURE 13-5:
The annual calendar display.

Setting Other Display Options

In addition to the default display option, you can set other personal preferences for the calendar on your phone. To get to the settings for the calendar, tap the More link on the daily, weekly, or monthly calendars and tap Settings. Doing so brings up the screen shown in Figure 13-6.

You have the following options:

>> **First day of week:** The standard in the United States is that a week is displayed from Sunday to Saturday. If you prefer the week to start on Saturday or Monday, you can change it here.

>> **Show week numbers:** Some people prefer to see the week number on the weekly calendar. If you count yourself among those, check this option.

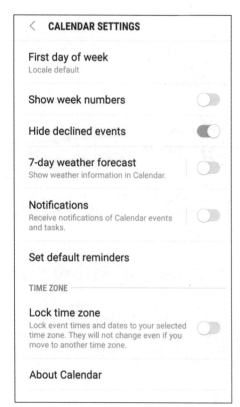

FIGURE 13-6:
The Settings
options for
the calendar
application.

>> **Hide declined events:** When some of us decline an event, we don't care to hear about it again. Others may want to keep a reminder of the declined event in case the situation changes (or in case nothing better comes along). The default setting is to hide declined events; if you want to see them, deselect this box.

>> **7-day weather forecast:** If you look at the monthly calendar shown in Figure 13-1, you can see an image on some of the days representing the weather forecast. If you like seeing this, you can keep this information. If you feel it takes too much real estate on your screen, you can delete it.

>> **Notification:** When an event is approaching, you can have the phone alert you with a pop-up, signal a notification on the status line, or do nothing. The default is to give you a notification, but you can change that option here.

>> **Set default reminders:** It helps some of us to be reminded about an appointment a few minutes before we are to be somewhere. Others of us find this annoying. This setting lets you choose whether you get a reminder or not and how far in advance you will be reminded.

>> **Lock time zone:** When you travel to a new time zone, your phone will take on the new time zone. Under most circumstances, this is a nice convenience. However, it may be confusing to some. If you prefer that the calendar remain in your home time zone, check this option.

Creating an Event on the Right Calendar

An important step in using a calendar when mobile is creating an event. It's even more important to make sure that the event ends up on the right calendar. This section covers the steps to make this happen.

Creating, editing, and deleting an event

Here's how to create an event — referred to as (well, yeah) an "event" — on your phone. Start from one of the calendar displays shown in Figures 13-1, 13-3, or 13-4. Tap the bright green circle with the plus (+) sign at the bottom right of the calendar. Doing so brings up the pop-up screen shown in Figure 13-7 (without the keyboard).

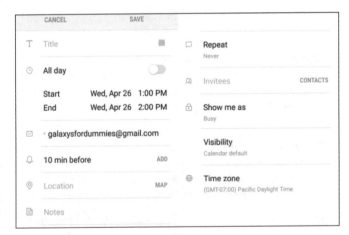

FIGURE 13-7:
The Create Event screen.

The only required information to get things started is a memorable event name and the Start and End times.

You need the following information at hand when making an event:

>> **Calendar:** Decide on which calendar you want to keep this event. Figure 13-7 shows that this event will be stored on the Gmail calendar. This is indicated by showing my Gmail account next to the blue dot in the middle of the screen. When you tap this selection, the phone presents you with the other calendars you've synced to your phone; you can store an event on any of them.

>> **Title:** Call the event something descriptive so that you can remember what it is without having to open it up.

>> **Start and End:** The two entry fields for the start and end times. Select the All Day toggle if the event is a full-day event.

>> **Notification:** This field lets you set how soon before an event your phone will alert you that you have an upcoming event. This makes it less likely that you'll be late to an appointment if you set this alert to accommodate your travel time.

>> **Location:** This setting ties in to the Google Maps app, allowing you to enter an address or a landmark. You can also just enter text.

If you want, you can enter more details on the meeting by adding the following:

>> **Repeat:** This option is useful for recurring events, such as weekly meetings.

>> **Invitees:** This allows you to have a group meeting by entering multiple contacts.

>> **Notes:** Add information that you find useful about that meeting.

>> **Privacy:** This is the same idea as the Show Me As option, but for non-Outlook-based calendars.

>> **Time zone:** If you and everyone that is invited will be in the same time zone, you are set. If you happen to be in another time zone or some of the invitees are in other time zones, you can use this option to ensure that you are not setting a meeting off business hours, or worse, in the middle of the night.

After you fill in the obligatory (and any optional) fields and settings, tap the Save link at the top of the page. The event is stored in whichever calendar you selected when you sync.

After you save an event, you can edit or delete it:

>> **Edit:** Open the event by tapping it from within one of the calendar views. This brings up the information as entered. Make your changes and tap Save. It's changed when it syncs.

>> **Delete:** To delete an event, start by tapping the entry on the screen. Tap the green Delete link at the top left. This brings up the pop-up as seen in Figure 13-8 to delete the event. Tap Delete. The event is gone.

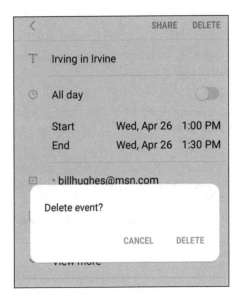

FIGURE 13-8:
The Delete
Event pop-up
screen.

TIP

You can also create an event by tapping the calendar itself twice. Tapping it twice brings up a pop-up (refer to Figure 13-7) where you can enter the event details.

Keeping events separate and private

When you have multiple calendars stored in one place (in this case, your phone), you might get confused when you want to add a new event. It can be even more confusing when you need to add the real event on one calendar and a placeholder on another.

Suppose your boss is a jerk and to retain your sanity, you need to find a new job. You send your resume to the arch-rival firm, Plan B, which has offices across town. Plan B is interested and wants to interview you at 3 p.m. next Tuesday. All good news.

The problem is that your current boss demands that you track your every move on the company calendaring system. His draconian management style is to berate people if they're not at their desks doing work when they're not at a scheduled meeting. (By the way, I am not making up this scenario.)

You follow my drift. You don't want Snidely Whiplash trudging through your calendar, sniffing out your plans to exit stage left, and making life more miserable if Plan B doesn't work out. Instead, you want to put a reasonable-sounding placeholder on your work calendar, while putting the real event on your personal calendar. You can easily do this from your calendar on your Samsung Galaxy S8. When you're making the event, you simply tell the phone where you want the event stored, making sure to keep each event exactly where it belongs.

The process begins with the Create Event screen. You bring this up by tapping the + sign in the green circle seen at the bottom-right corner of any of the calendars seen in Figures 13-1, 13-3, or 13-4. The information for the real event is shown on the left in Figure 13-9. The fake event is shown on the right. This is the one that is saved to your work email. The colored dot by the work address helps you be aware that this is a different calendar.

Real Appointment on Phone

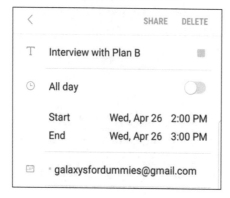

Fake Appointment on Work Email

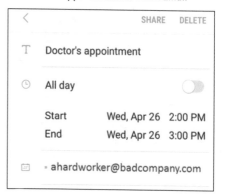

FIGURE 13-9:
The Add an Event screen on your phone.

Now, when you look at your calendar on your phone, you see two events at the same time. (Check it out in Figure 13-10.) The Galaxy S8 doesn't mind if you make two simultaneous events.

Under the circumstances, this is what you wanted to create. As long as your boss doesn't see your phone, you're safe — to try to find more fulfilling employment, that is.

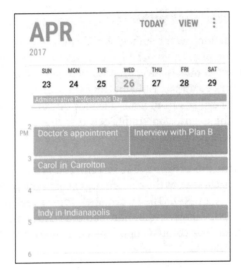

FIGURE 13-10:
Two events on
the same day
on your phone
calendar.

Chapter **14**

Talking with Bixby

ixby is Samsung's new effort to offer an intelligent agent. The purpose of an intelligent agent is to anticipate your questions and get information faster. It typically involves simply speaking to your phone and having it do what you're asking without having to tap or type.

Earlier devices had S-Voice. Now you have Bixby, and Bixby is powerful. However, if you're one of the first buyers of the Samsung Galaxy S8, you may need to wait a while for voice recognition. Sorry. The other parts of Bixby, called Bixby Home and Bixby Vision, are very powerful and will do for now.

Bringing Up Bixby

The Bixby home page is all about getting you summaries of the information you want to see the most in the most efficient way for you. The Bixby home page gives you summaries of information from a variety of different apps. Each summary is called a *Bixby card.*

There are two ways to access the Bixby Home page:

» Press the Bixby button on the left side of the phone twice.

» Swipe to the right from the Home screen.

Take either of these actions and you see the Bixby home page, shown in Figure 14-1.

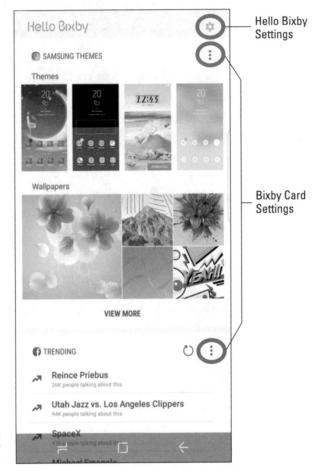

Hello Bixby
Settings

Bixby Card
Settings

FIGURE 14-1:
The Bixby
home page.

You can have as many or as few cards as you want on the Bixby home page. You can see all the options for setting up cards by tapping the Hello Bixby Settings icon, shown in the upper-right corner of Figure 14-1. This brings up the list of Bixby-supported apps (see Figure 14-2).

When you tap supported apps, you can see all the apps that you could potentially put on your Bixby page (Figure 14-3). This includes apps you've already downloaded, as well as apps that you may want to download. This list will continue to change as more apps support the Bixby card. If you see an app is supported, but you haven't downloaded it yet, simply tap the Download button, and you'll be taken to the page within the Google Play Store so you can add it immediately.

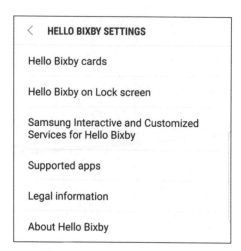

FIGURE 14-2:
The Bixby
Settings page.

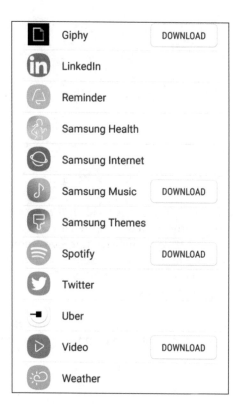

FIGURE 14-3:
The apps
supported
by Bixby.

You add a card for this application by tapping the Hello Bixby Cards link on the Bixby Settings page (refer to Figure 14-2). This will bring up the page shown in Figure 14-4.

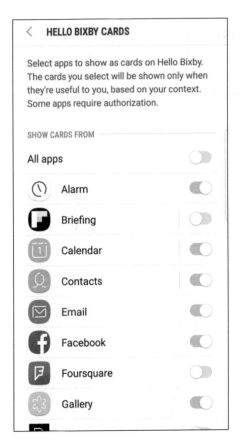

FIGURE 14-4:
Active Bixby
cards.

If the toggle switch is to the right and shows blue, it means there is a card for it on the Bixby home page. If the switch is to the left, this app does not have a card on the Bixby home page. If you want to add it, you simply slide the switch to the right. If you want to delete the card, you simply slide the switch to the left. Figure 14-5 shows the Bixby home page in panorama if you tap the toggle to have all apps have cards on the Bixby home page.

You have some flexibility in the placement of the cards. Each card has three vertical dots in the upper-right corner. When you tap these dots, you get the pop-up shown in Figure 14-6.

If you're particularly interested in one card, you can tap Pin to Top. This will move that card to the top of the list. You can also choose to hide a given card or remove it from the Bixby page.

FIGURE 14-5:
When all apps have active Bixby cards.

| Pin to top |
| Hide for now |
| Don't show again |
| Settings |

FIGURE 14-6:
Display options for each Bixby card.

The Bixby page is very handy when you're actively using your phone. You can also see Bixby cards when the lock screen is active. If you're simply looking for the temperature, the score of the game, or if a message has arrived, and it's inconvenient or inappropriate to unlock your phone, you're in luck. Back in the Bixby Settings screen, tap Hello Bixby on Lock Screen. Choose the cards that you want to be able to see without unlocking your phone. When you press the Bixby button twice, you'll see the information on the selected cards and nothing for the cards that were not selected on the screen (see Figure 14-7).

The left image is what you see when the phone is unlocked and select Bixby. In this case, you see the cards for the calendar and Facebook. The right image is what you see if you press the Bixby button when the phone is locked. In this case, you can see an upcoming appointment, but nothing about Facebook. It's entirely up to you what cards you see and when.

Bixby Screen when phone is unlocked

Bixby Screen when phone is locked

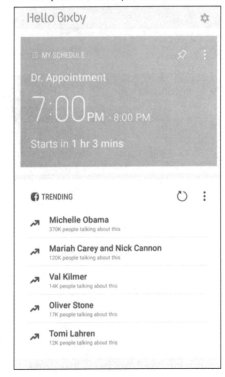

FIGURE 14-7:
Bixby cards
when the
phone is
unlocked and
locked.

Visualizing What You Can Do with Bixby Vision

In Chapter 9, I point out the Bixby icon in the viewfinder. You can see it here in the margin. When you have the camera app open, you can tap the icon to launch Bixby Vision. Bixby Vision can then tell you information about what the camera is pointed at:

>> If it's an object, Bixby Vision can tell you what the object is and how much you can buy it for online.

>> If it's a barcode or QR code, Bixby Vision can tell you what the code means.

>> If it's text, Bixby Vision can read it and convert it to text. You can then translate that text into any of 108 languages.

>> If it's a landmark, Bixby Vision can tell you where it's located.

>> If it's a wine label, Bixby Vision can tell you the ranking of the wine and what food pairs well with it.

How Bixby Vision works is simple. You open the camera application and point the camera so that it has a good view of the object, document, barcode, text, or wine label just as described back in Chapter 9 (see Figure 14-8).

Normal camera viewfinder   Camera viewfinder with
                                      Bixby Vision

FIGURE 14-8:
A typical
image from
the Viewfinder
before and
after tapping
Bixby Vision.

When you tap the Bixby icon on the viewfinder, your phone starts trying to figure out what you want. In Figure 14-8, it sees an apple and then asks you whether you want it to search this object as an image to find out what it is or whether you're interested in shopping for this item. Let's say that I want to buy an apple. I tap the Shopping icon. The results are in Figure 14-9.

So, I really wanted to get prices on fresh honey crisp apples from the state of Washington. I guess apple-flavored jelly beans are reasonably close.

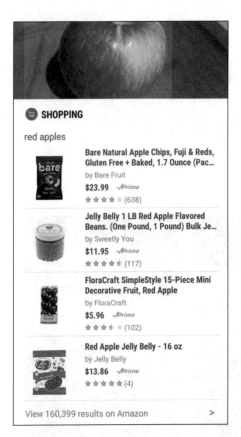

FIGURE 14-9:
Shopping
options
presented
based on
Figure 14-8.

The point is that Bixby Vision does its best to interpret what you want. In Figure 14-8, you see that it presents two icons: one to identify the object and the other giving you shopping alternatives. Currently, there are six options for icons (see Figure 14-10).

FIGURE 14-10:
Bixby Vision
icons that may
pop up.

Bixby will present one or more of these icons based on what it thinks is in the image and what you want. Not only is this fun, but you might save some money when you're shopping!

Blabbing with Bixby

Every science-fiction movie worth its salt predicts a world where we speak to computers rather than typing in data. Normal conversation is about 150 words per minute, whereas even an expert typist can only type at 90 words per minute. More important, talking is the most basic form of communication. The reality is that there are many technical obstacles to having voice recognition match the ideal of a computer perfectly interpreting the meaning of any user's verbal instructions.

That does not stop us from having some fun in the meantime. When Bixby includes Voice, you'll be able to make a phone call, send an email or a text, search the web, or even update your Facebook status and calendar with voice commands.

You may love this capability, or you may find it to be a gimmick and not very useful. Either way, you can have some fun with this.

Look Ma! No Hands!

Say you want to call someone.

In the old days, high-end mobile phones would require you to train the voice-recognition software to understand the basics of how you speak. No more. Just tell it who you want to call, by saying, "Call Bill."

Be ready. In just a moment, it calls Bill. It's that easy.

However, if you know several people named Bill, your phone asks you (in a semi-pleasant voice) which "Bill" you want to call.

You may have heard of "Siri" on the iPhone. Siri responds to questions you ask it. The Bixby app is the same idea, except it responds to the name "Bixby."

If you want to call Bill Boyce, a person from your contact list, say "Call Bill Boyce." Within a moment, his phone rings.

A few pointers for using Bixby. If you hesitate, Bixby assumes that you are not ready to talk and goes into a sleep mode. To wake it up, just say "Hi, Bixby." It wakes up, ready to resume listening.

I get to the list of things that work with Bixby soon. For now, try a few of its simple-yet-valuable capabilities.

Dictating a Text

To send a text, say the words, "Send a text." Done. The text screen pops up.

Bixby asks you, "Who would you like to message?" Give the name. It looks up their number from your contact list. In Figure 14-3, I have said the name "Ludwig van Beethoven." Bixby then asks you for your message. Go ahead and say what you would have typed.

Bixby then converts your words into a message. It displays what it thinks you said in a box similar to the box shown in Figure 14-11.

Read it before you send it. If it is correct, just say "Send" and off it goes. If it's incorrect, you can say "Cancel," and it won't send that message. You can then try again.

FIGURE 14-11:
The text prepared by Bixby, ready to go.

Preparing to Work with Bixby

Texting is a straightforward example, but it is just one of the tasks Bixby can do for you. You can ask Bixby to do all kinds of things on your phone. Some examples include

>> Telling you the time

>> Setting an alarm

>> Turning Wi-Fi on or off

>> Telling you the weather forecast

>> Setting a countdown timer

>> Recording your voice

>> Opening an app

>> Playing a playlist

>> Adding an appointment to your schedule

>> Finding a local restaurant, store, or public location

>> Navigating to an address or location

All you need to do is ask, and Bixby does a good job finding what you want. For example, you can ask for a nearby McDonald's, and Bixby comes back with some options, as shown in Figure 14-12.

FIGURE 14-12:
Bixby options
on a location.

Then you can ask it for directions to the McDonald's you choose. This request causes Bixby to hand you over to your preferred navigation application, bringing up a screen like the one shown in Figure 14-13.

Now all you need to do is drive there safely and enjoy!

FIGURE 14-13:
Navigating to
the location
you requested.

A WORD ABOUT INTELLIGENT AGENTS

Among computer scientists, Bixby is called an *intelligent agent*.

Bixby is a pretty darn good implementation of intelligent-agent technology. The list of things you can do with Bixby includes a pretty long list of the capabilities.

Even so, the truth is that this technology is not perfected yet. As you see in this chapter, I wanted to buy a fresh apple and that isn't exactly what Bixby presented. If you don't want to use an intelligent agent until it's perfected, no one could blame you. Before you dismiss this function as a gimmick, however, here are a few things to remember:

- Normal speech communicates ideas at about 150 words per minute.
- A fast typist can type at 90 words per minute.
- In handwriting, most people can write 30 words per minute.

These data show that you and I may be better off if we can adjust our expectations of asking computers to do things for us by speaking to them. If you use Bixby for standard commands, it performs remarkably fast and accurately. You will get to say to your grandkids that you were among the pioneers who used intelligent agents before it was mainstream.

As long as evil intelligent agent, HAL, from *2001: A Space Odyssey* never comes to pass, it's likely that this technology will become increasingly pervasive.

Chapter **15**

Paying with Samsung Pay

S omeday in the future, you will be able to leave your wallet at home and just use your smartphone for all the stuff that you carry with you today. We are not there yet, but Samsung has implemented some technology that moves us toward that day.

You may reasonably ask why not carrying your wallet is such a big deal. Fair enough. The two main reasons are that it is more convenient and more secure. Samsung Pay takes us a long way to this ultimate goal. The reality is you will need to continue to carry your wallet with credit cards and cash for now.

For now, you'll need to decide for yourself whether the convenience that Samsung Pay does offer is worth the effort associated with setting it up. Samsung has gone to great lengths to make transactions more secure than simply using a credit card. Like so many of these things, the security is only as good as how the individual implements it.

With that awareness, some things about Samsung Pay are exceptionally cool. If you like to show off new technology to people, this is a good opportunity. In particular, you can one-up your smug friends who use Apple Pay with their iPhones. That capability alone is worth the price of admission for some of us.

How Mobile Payment Works

It helps to explain how mobile payments work to see how Samsung Pay helps you. The idea is that you walk up to the checkout stand at a retailer. You swipe your fingerprint on the reader, place your phone near the card reader, and instantly your transaction is done. The receipt prints, and you take your purchase and go on your merry way. The charge shows up on your credit card.

Besides a fingerprint, you can enter a four-digit PIN or a quick retinal scan by glancing at your phone. You choose the security option that is most convenient for you, and Samsung makes sure that everything flows securely. All the authorizations were set up when you set up the credit card with Samsung Pay.

Really. That's all there is.

It sounds so simple. The interesting thing is that this capability has been around in one form or another for almost 20 years. Back in 1997, Mobil gas stations implemented contactless payment with their Speedpass. Users on the system would tap their Speedpass fobs that they would keep on the key ring on the reader installed on the gas pump.

Their credit card would be charged for the gas they pumped. Initially, the tap was all that it took to pay for the gas. Later, users needed to add their ZIP code to enhance security. In spite of Mobil's best efforts, the system had only moderate success. There are a range of reasons, but a major concern was that people were already hesitant to even carry yet another thing. It is the inclusion of some new technology within smartphones that makes it so much more convenient.

Visa and MasterCard also tried contactless systems with limited success. One of their major challenges is that not enough credit card readers support the contactless payment system. After years of trying, fewer than 10 percent of all credit card readers as recently as 2015 have this capability. Those readers that do support contactless payment have the logo shown in Figure 15-1.

FIGURE 15-1:
The contactless payment logo.

The contactless payment approach got a significant boost when Apple introduced the Apple Pay system on the iPhone in 2014. Like some other technologies that have struggled to find widespread acceptance, the implementation by Apple produces enough momentum that overcomes any resistance to its widespread use.

Examples include the Apple Macintosh with its use of a mouse, the Apple iPod revolutionizing the acceptance of MP3 players, and the Apple iPad creating a revolutionizing a trend for tablets. All of these technologies were pioneered by other companies before Apple made them popular.

The Apple Pay system has seen significant success in an area where others have struggled. The retailers with the contactless credit card technology have seen a huge increase in its use from iPhone customers.

With Samsung Pay, however, Samsung has leapfrogged Apple. Samsung Pay works similarly to Apple Pay with contactless payment devices. It also works with the vast majority of standard credit card readers. Take that, Apple!

While 10 percent of credit card readers in retailers today support contactless payment, another 85 percent of credit card readers at retailers have readers that can read the magnetic stripe on the back of your credit card. Samsung Pay along with your Galaxy S8 have the electronics built in to work with the contactless system but also the electronics to convince the magnetic stripe readers that you have swiped your card!

TECHNICAL
STUFF

The technology within your phone that works with the standard credit card readers is called *Magnetic Secure Transmission,* or MST. When you place your phone near the magnetic stripe reader, it sends a very short range signal to the magnetic stripe reader on your card that simulates the signals it gets when you physically swipe a magnetic stripe reader.

Your imagination could go wild and come up with ways that fiendish people could potentially steal this technology. One can never say never, but there are extensive procedures that are put in place to set up this capability to prevent it in most instances. The rest of this chapter walks you through those processes.

TIP

Probably the biggest drawback in using this technology these days is that too few retail clerks know that it will work. They freak out the first time they see it as they are probably familiar with contactless payment methods, know that they do not have it, and do not know about this slick solution. They will want to ask you more about it, which will end up taking more time than if you were paying by writing a check and having to provide two forms of identification!

Getting Started with Samsung Pay

The first step in the process is to make sure that you have Samsung Pay on your Galaxy S8. As cool as this app is, there are many options to this technology, and your carrier may have preferred to not have it preloaded. No problem. Chapter 8 explains how to download applications from the Play Store. The Samsung Pay logo is seen in Figure 15-2.

FIGURE 15-2:
The Samsung Pay and the Android Pay logos.

TIP

It is easy to confuse Samsung Pay and Android Pay. These are two different applications. Android Pay is nice, but it does not have the Magnetic Secure Transmission capability that allows you to use mobile payments at many more retailers.

The app page description is shown in Figure 15-3. When you tap Install, you get the image on the right.

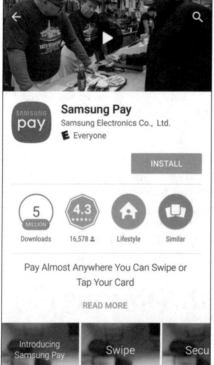
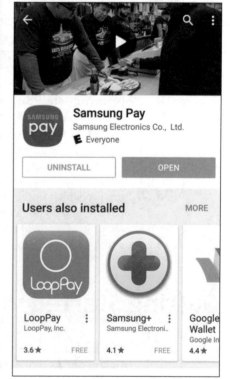

FIGURE 15-3:
The Samsung Pay app Play Store images before and after installation.

The Samsung Pay app works a little different than most other apps. The first time you open Samsung Pay, you will be given information on how to use it and be asked to put in your credit card information (in a very convenient way, by the way) and asked all kinds of permissions and agreements.

Once you have given all this information, Samsung Pay waits patiently at the bottom of your home pages, ready to meet your payment needs with nothing more than a quick swipe from the bottom of the screen. Most people would simply not use this app if they had to go digging through their screens to find the app. This way, you do not have to search to find the app and wait for it to come up.

Figure 15-4 shows the Lock screen with the Samsung Pay launch button sitting at the bottom ready to appear with a quick flick.

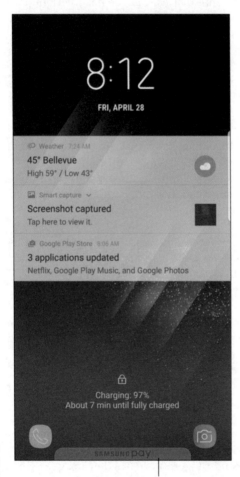

FIGURE 15-4:
The Samsung
Pay quick
launch button.

Samsung Pay quick launch button

The launch button is also there on the Home screen, but is not visible when running other applications.

Setting Up Samsung Pay

When you open the app, you're greeted with a series of pages before you get to the Home screen seen in Figure 15-4. These pages include marketing introductions (which you don't need because you read this chapter), permissions and agreements (which you should give if you want to move forward), and some pages that verify that Samsung Pay can work on your phone.

The app wants to make sure that your phone has the right parts (your Galaxy S8 does, but that is not the case for every Android phone) and that you are in one of the 15 countries where Samsung Pay is accepted. You're set if you're in the United States, Canada, Puerto Rico, or China. You're out of luck if you're in, say, Yemen. Being in these countries is important for this app because each country has its own set of laws for payments, and Samsung may not have all the arrangements in place if you are not in one of these countries. New countries will be added as quickly as possible.

TIP

Read the agreements. In all likelihood, they are the same kind of agreements that exist in the fine print in your existing credit card and every time you sign your name to a credit card charge slip that affirms you won't pull any shenanigans. That said, I am your humble author, not your legal advisor, and you should feel comfortable with these agreements.

The next part of the initial setup process is to step through how you want to set up security. You have three security options when you are making a transaction: using your fingerprint, using a retinal scan, or entering a PIN. Figure 15-5 shows the screen that gives you the option.

There are a few scenarios where using a Samsung Pay PIN rather than a fingerprint might make sense. In most cases, using your fingerprint or eye scan is exceptionally convenient. Chapter 17 describes the process for using these biometric options as a security method. If you've already set these up in your phone, you see Figure 15-6. If you haven't set these up yet, the Samsung Pay application will walk you through the steps to do so. It's quick and easy.

The next step is to enter your credit card information. When you tap the link that says Add Card, you will be taken to a screen that lets you take an image of your credit card. This is seen in Figure 15-7. The left image is when the screen first comes up and the right image is when you have the desired credit card in the viewfinder.

FIGURE 15-5:
The Samsung
Pay security
option
selection page.

FIGURE 15-6:
The Samsung
Pay credit card
preparation
page.

Before taking an image of your card

After taking an image of your card

FIGURE 15-7:
The Samsung
Pay credit
card image
processing
screen.

Viewfinder

The app then interprets the information on the front of your credit card and populates as many screens as possible with your credit card information. It will ask you to fill out the form seen in Figure 15-8 if it can't figure out the information on your card or the information is on the reverse side of the card.

TIP

Not every company that offers credit cards is signed up with Samsung Pay. You can check the Samsung website or tap the link in Figure 15-7 to check before you proceed. Otherwise, just go ahead and see whether things go through.

Tap Next, and Samsung Pay will seek to confirm things with your credit card company. This does not cost you anything. It just wants to make sure that when you do make a charge, everything will flow smoothly. One of the things the company will want to verify is that you are authorized to use that credit card. This means that either you need to be the primary cardholder or you need to coordinate with that person. The screen seen in Figure 15-9 comes up.

There are three credit card verification options. If you tap SMS, it will send a code to the primary cardholder's mobile phone. You then enter the code in the next screen and you're verified.

FIGURE 15-8:
The Populated credit card data fields.

FIGURE 15-9:
Credit card verification screen.

If you tap email, the bank offering the credit card will send an email to the primary cardholder's email address. Again, you enter the code sent in the next screen.

The last option is that the primary cardholder calls the customer service line at the bank and makes the request to connect to Samsung Pay.

Once you are verified, it is possible that your phone will ask you to verify that you want to make Samsung Pay your primary app. This is seen in Figure 15-10. (Never let it be said that the folks at Google did not try hard to get you to use Android Pay.)

You're almost there. The next screen, seen in Figure 15-11, is for you to enter your signature if you're using a credit card or your PIN if you're using a debit card.

Keep in mind that scanning your fingerprint and tapping your phone on a credit card reader has the same legal implications as actually signing a credit slip.

Once everything is ready, you get the verification screen seen in Figure 15-12.

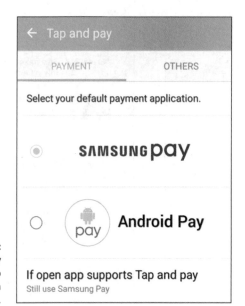

FIGURE 15-10:
Tap and pay
primary app
verification
screen.

FIGURE 15-11:
Signature
screen.

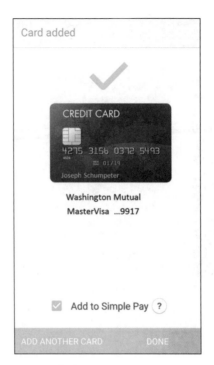

FIGURE 15-12:
Card added
verification
screen.

Using Samsung Pay

First, pick something to buy at a store. Have a clerk ring it up and tell him you will pay with a credit card. Swipe the screen upward. You see the screen seen in Figure 15-13.

Tap the security option you want to employ, and you see a screen similar to Figure 15-14.

As seen in Figure 15-14, you should either hold your phone against where the credit card reader would read the magnetic stripe or where there is the contactless payment system logo if it is available.

The semicircle above your signature will start counting down, and your phone will vibrate to let you know that it is transmitting. You will hear a beep if it all goes through. If it fails for some reason, you can try again simply by reentering your security option.

FIGURE 15-13:
Samsung
Pay payment
screen before
reading
security option.

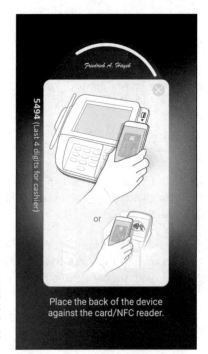

FIGURE 15-14:
Samsung
Pay payment
screen after
reading
fingerprint.

TIP

This process works with the vast majority of credit card readers. This does not work well, however, with credit card readers where you insert your card into the machine and pull it out quickly. This type of reader is mostly used on gasoline pumps. Sorry.

Managing Samsung Pay

As long as you pay your credit card bills and keep your credit card account at the bank, this app is relatively self-sufficient. Still, you will need to access the app settings from time to time. You get there by tapping the Samsung Pay logo in the upper-left corner of the payment screen that you see in Figure 15-13. This will bring up the screen similar to what you see in Figure 15-15.

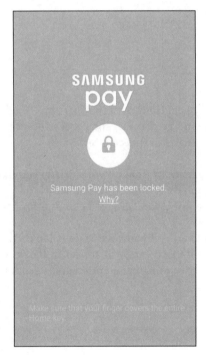

FIGURE 15-15:
Samsung
Pay settings
security
screen.

This is a security screen to keep anyone who doesn't have your fingerprint or your eyes (which is you and only you) away from the actual settings. Have it read your selected biometric, and you get to the page seen in Figure 15-16.

FIGURE 15-16:
Samsung
Pay settings
security
screen.

Now this looks like a more typical Home screen of an app. To add a new credit or debit card, tap the Add link and go through the process described in the section "Setting Up Samsung Pay," earlier in this chapter.

Adding a second card is easy, and the images will stack up when above each other on this page. The quick launch link brings up whatever card is on the top. If you want to change to use a different credit card, you can flip through the options.

If you want to delete a credit card, all you have to do is tap on the card image. All the information associated with that card will appear in the screen. You have the opportunity to delete it by tapping the menu option and selecting Delete.

Enjoy your spending!

6

The Part of Tens

IN THIS PART . . .

Get the most out of your phone.

Protect yourself if you lose your phone.

Avoid losing your phone in the first place.

Discover what features will be coming in future versions.

» **Checking out the extra cool features that make this phone so good**

» **Making a personal statement**

Chapter **16**

Ten Ways to Make Your Phone Totally Yours

A smartphone is a very personal device. From the moment you take it out of the box and strip off the packaging, you begin to make it yours. By the end of the first day, even though millions of your type of phone may have been sold, there's no other phone just like yours.

This is the case because of the phone calls you make and because of all the options you can set on the phone and all the information you can share over the web. Your contacts, music files, downloaded videos, texts, and favorites make your phone a unique representation of who you are and what's important to you.

Even with all this "you" on your phone, this chapter covers ten or so ways to further customize your phone beyond what this book covers. Some of these suggestions involve accessories. Others involve settings and configurations. All are worth considering.

When it comes to accessories, your carrier's retail store has many good options. And oodles, heaps, loads, and tons of options for your phone are available outside the carrier's retail store. There is no need to limit yourself.

Using a Bluetooth Speaker

In just a matter of a couple of years, Bluetooth speakers have gone from an interesting (and expensive) option to mainstream. Prices have come down quickly, and the variety of designs for the speakers has grown dramatically. In all cases, you get the benefit of being able to play your music on your phone without the inconvenience of having headphones. You also get a speakerphone, although the quality of the audio can vary dramatically from Bluetooth speaker to Bluetooth speaker.

This accessory is best purchased in a brick-and-mortar store where you can listen to a variety of choices. Although syncing with a number of speaker choices can be tedious, it's the only way you'll know if a particular Bluetooth speaker meets your needs.

Although sound quality is essential, the folks in the industrial-design department have been having a lot of fun coming up with ways for the Bluetooth speaker to look. Figure 16-1 shows a range of options for the most popular form factors.

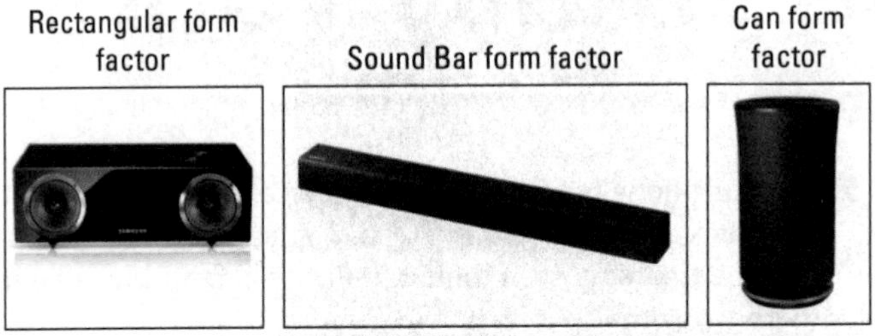

Rectangular form factor   Sound Bar form factor   Can form factor

FIGURE 16-1: Popular Bluetooth speaker form factors.

The most popular options are basically a rectangle, the can style, and the sound bar. Each company has its own twist, but these options represent what you can see in the high-volume stores.

Fortunately, you live in a world where designers can get creative. Figure 16-2 shows some of the more exceptional designs.

The House of Marley, for example, uses unconventional design and recycled material to stand out in the market. CRAZY BABY makes the Mars series, which includes a levitating speaker. SPI Home produces a Bluetooth speaker built into a variety of garden statues, including a pelican.

There is no shortage of imagination when it comes to Bluetooth. Be sure to consider all your options. Before you settle on the mainstream options at the local mall, do some research off the beaten path. You'll be amazed at the range of options.

House of Marley

CRAZY BABY
levitating speaker

SPI-Home Pelican
speaker

FIGURE 16-2:
Unusual
designs for
Bluetooth
speakers.

Cruising in the Car

You may have gotten the idea that I am concerned about your safety when you're using your phone. True, but I'm also concerned with *my* safety when you're using your phone. I would like you to have a Bluetooth speaker in your car when driving in my neighborhood, if you please.

Some cars have a built-in Bluetooth system within the car stereo that connects to a microphone somewhere on the dash as well as to your car speakers. It's smart enough to sense an incoming call and mutes your music in response.

If you don't have such a setup, there are lots of good options for car speakers. Figure 16-3 shows an example.

FIGURE 16-3:
Bluetooth car
speaker.

A closely related accessory is a car mount. A *car mount* will hold your phone in a place you can easily observe as you drive. The mount attaches to an air vent, the dashboard, or the windshield.

You could always put your phone on the seat next to you, but that's for amateurs. Instead, offer your phone a place of honor with a car docking station. It makes accessing your phone while you drive safer and easier. Some see getting a car mount as a luxury, but my view is that if you need to upgrade your navigation software, you need a vehicle mount.

WARNING

Be sure to put away the docking station when you park. Even an empty docking station is a lure for a thief.

Figure 16-4 shows the Samsung Vehicle Navigation Mount. It costs about $100, and you can get it at your carrier's store, RadioShack, Best Buy, or online at Amazon.com. It includes a wireless charging pad.

FIGURE 16-4:
The Samsung Vehicle Navigation Mount.

More economical vehicle mounts are available that do not include a wireless charging pad. Figure 16-5 shows an example from SlipGrip that costs closer to $30.

FIGURE 16-5:
A SlipGrip vehicle mount.

This version is special because it is specifically designed to work with larger protective cases. It can be a hassle to have to remove the protective case from your phone to insert it in a vehicle mount. In addition to a car mount, SlipGrip also offers a mount for your bicycle.

TIP

When shopping for a car mount or a bike mount, be sure to consider the extra girth associated with a case. If you don't use a case (which is a mistake), you just need to be sure that the mount is compatible with a Galaxy S8. If you have a case on your phone (which is anything but a mistake), be sure the mount will work with the Galaxy S8 *and* the case.

Considering Wireless Charging Mats

Those industrial designers have certainly gone crazy with Bluetooth speakers. They have also been having a field day on wireless charging options. For example, the Samsung Vehicle Navigation Mount shown in Figure 16-4 has a built-in charger.

Most wireless charging mats are designed with the idea that you can place your phone on the mat, and technology will do the rest. You can get a standard Samsung wireless charging pad, shown in Figure 16-6, for about $50. Samsung also offers the Fast Charging pad, which will charge your phone from stone-cold dead to 100 percent in just a few hours. This capability costs a little more, closer to $70.

FIGURE 16-6:
The Samsung wireless charging pad (left) and the Samsung Fast Charging pad (right).

If these are too conventional for you, more options are out there as well. Figure 16-7 shows some of the more interesting options. You can go colorful, high-tech, or back to nature. Your choice.

TYLT wireless
charging stand

Luna Qi charger

Wood charging
stand

FIGURE 16-7:
More exotic wireless charging pads.

Look for more options going forward!

Using a Keyboard Cover

One feature that some people just cannot get over is having tactile feedback from a keyboard, even a real keyboard. This harkens back to the day when Blackberry was the "it" phone.

Fear not! Samsung has a solution for you with the Galaxy S8. It's called the Keyboard Cover (see Figure 16-8), and it snaps onto your S8. Your phone knows it's there and covering part of the screen, and the phone immediately condenses everything to the top part of the screen. When you remove the keyboard cover, you get the whole screen back automatically. This product is ingenious.

FIGURE 16-8:
The Keyboard Cover from Samsung.

Ingenious, yes, but there are two things to keep in mind:

>> It only works with the S8 and not the S8+.

>> Unlike your old Blackberry, the keys are not backlit.

Making a Statement with Wraps

Not the sandwich kind of wraps. I'm talking about the kind of wrap that lets you customize the non-glass portion of the S8.

The Samsung Galaxy S8 is very attractive, but you can spruce it up with an adhesive covering called a wrap from Skinit at `www.skinit.com`. These designs can express more of what is important to you. As a side benefit, they can protect your phone from minor scratches.

Figure 16-9 shows some design options for a skin. It comes with cut-outs for speakers, plugs, microphones, and cameras specifically for the Galaxy S8. Putting the skin on is similar to putting on a decal, although it has a little give in the material to make positioning easier. The skin material and adhesive are super high-tech and have enough give to allow klutzes like me (who struggle with placing regular decals) to fit the nooks and crannies of the phone like an expert.

GALAXY S8 SKINS

   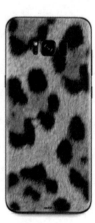

FIGURE 16-9:
Some sample
wrap designs.

The Few The Proud Camo Marines   Distressed American Flag

van Gogh - The Starry Night

Leopard

If you're not crazy about Skinit's designs, you can make your own with images of your own choosing. Just be sure that you have the rights to use the images!

You Look Wonderful: Custom Screen Images

In addition to the shortcuts on your extended Home screen, you can also customize the images that are behind the screen. You can change the background to one of three options:

>> Choose a neutral background image (similar to the backgrounds on many PCs) from the Wallpaper Gallery. Figure 16-10 shows a selection of background images that are standard on your phone.

>> Any picture from your Gallery can be virtually stretched across the seven screens of your home page. (Read more about the Gallery in Chapter 9.)

>> Opt for a theme that changes the background and fonts.

FIGURE 16-10: Standard wallpaper sample images.

The pictures from your Gallery and the Wallpaper Gallery are images that you can set by pressing and holding the Home screen. In a moment, you see icons appear. Select Wallpapers and pick the image you want.

The themes take it to a different level. In addition to the background, the phone will change the fonts and many of the basic icons. You see the themes in Figure 16-11 that are based upon European landscapes, if that's your thing. (There are lots of options if it isn't.)

FIGURE 16-11:
European
landscape
options.

A few samples also come on your phone. You may be a pink kind of person or a space nut. If these options aren't to your taste, tap the Store link at the top of the page to see a range of options. If you do not see one you like today, be sure to check back as developers are adding new themes all the time.

Empowering Power Savings

Imagine that you're flying on a short hop from Smallville to Littleton. You are about to take off when air traffic control tells the pilot that the plane needs to wait on the tarmac. Unfortunately, you are low on battery. The pilot says that it is okay to use your mobile phone.

Because you do not know how long this will take, you pull out your phone, go to Settings, and tap Battery. From here, you put it in Power Savings Mode. This slows down a lot of cool features. For example, it dims the screen, slows the processors and mobile data speeds, and kills the vibration mode. This extends the battery life with minor sacrifices to what you can do with your phone. The apps all run, but perhaps not as fast.

Then the pilot says that your plane has a flat tire, the maintenance crew went home, and you could be sitting there for hours.

This time you open Settings, tap Device Savings, tap Battery, and put your phone in Max Power Savings Mode. Your beautiful, powerful smartphone has instantly turned itself into a dumb feature phone. You won't be able to watch a full-length feature film. However, you now have enough battery to make and take phone calls and text messages for hours. This is not an exact science and your mileage may vary, but switching to this mode can multiply the time your smartphone can operate as a phone by eight to ten times.

Controlling Your Home Electronics

Traditional home appliances are getting smarter, offering more capabilities for better performance. One problem they have is that adding rows of control buttons (so that you can control those new capabilities) complicates manufacture. So, the next generation of appliances has begun to add a small LCD screen to the appliance. This can look slick, but it costs a lot and is prone to breakage. Also, the fancy capabilities involve pushing a confusing combination of buttons with cryptic messages displayed on a tiny screen.

The latest idea is to omit the screen altogether and give you control of the settings through an application on your smartphone. Your appliance retains the very basic buttons but allows you to use the fancy capabilities by setting them through your phone. You just download the free application made by the manufacturer from the Google Play Store, and you have your beautiful and logical user interface to control your new product — no strings attached.

For example, your new oven will allow you to turn it on and set the temperature without using a smartphone. However, if you want it to start preheating at 5:30 p.m. so that you can put the casserole in right when you walk in the door, you can set that up through your phone.

Wearing Wearables

Wearables are a class of mobile accessories that have been getting a lot of attention lately. For the most part, wearables are connected via Bluetooth and typically worn as a watch, although you can wear some sensors in athletic shoes. Samsung offers its wearables under the brand name Gear (see Figure 16-12).

Gear 3 Classic   Gear 3 Frontier

FIGURE 16-12:
Samsung Gear
wearables.

In addition to telling the time, these wearables give you notifications, weather, and texts and track some relevant information, such as the amount of exercise you've done. These images look like conventional, but stylish analog watches. When you rotate the bezel on the watch face, it shows you texts, a phone dialing pad, your altitude, and the useful information that would otherwise be shown on your phone. How cool is that?!

Using Your Phone as a PC

Your phone has all the computing power of a PC. Wouldn't it be nice if you didn't have to carry a laptop? Enter the Samsung Dex (see Figure 16-13).

FIGURE 16-13:
Samsung
Dex Docking
Station with
screen, mouse,
and keyboard.

The Dex Docking Station may look like a conventional charging station, but it's so much more. When you put your phone on the docking station, you can use a full keyboard, mouse, and screen as if it were a PC! The docking station has an Ethernet jack, two USB ports to support a keyboard and a mouse, and an HDMI port to connect to a full screen. What you plug it all in, you get the full functionality of a desktop. This is much smaller and more convenient than lugging around even the lightest laptop.

Chapter **17**

Ten (Or So) Ways to Make Your Phone Secure

B ack in the "old" days, it sure was frustrating to have your regular-feature phone lost or stolen. You would lose all your contacts, call history, and texts. Even if you backed up all your contacts, you would have to reenter them in your new phone. What a hassle.

WARNING

The good news is that your smartphone saves all your contacts on your email accounts. The bad news is that, unless you take some steps outlined in this chapter, evildoers could conceivably drain your bank account, get you fired, or even have you arrested.

Do I have your attention? Think of what would happen if someone were to get access to your PC at home or at work. He or she could wreak havoc on your life.

A malevolent prankster could send an email from your work email address under your name. It could be a rude note to the head of your company. It could give phony information about a supposedly imminent financial collapse of your company to the local newspaper. It could be a threat to the U.S. president, generating a visit from the Secret Service.

Here's the deal: If you have done anything with your smartphone as described in this book past Chapter 3, I expect you'll want to take steps to protect your smartphone. This is the burden of having a well-connected device. Fortunately, most of the steps are simple and straightforward.

Using a Good Case and Screen Cover

The Samsung Galaxy S8 is sleek and beautiful. The Galaxy S8 Edge has a really cool design that draws attention from people walking by. Plus, the front is made of Gorilla Glass from Corning. This stuff is super-durable and scratch-resistant.

So why am I telling you to cover this all up? It's like buying a fancy dress for a prom or wedding and wearing a coat all night. Yup. It's necessary for safe mobile computing.

WARNING

Speaking from personal experience, dropping a Galaxy phone on concrete can break the glass and some of the innards. This can happen if you simply keep your phone in a pocket.

There are lots of choices for cases. The most popular are made of silicone, plastic, or leather. There are different styles that meet your needs from many manufacturers. Otterbox is a brand that makes a series of cases for multiple levels of protection. The Defender Series for the Galaxy S8, its highest level of protection, is seen in black in Figure 17-1. You can get other levels of protection with more colors if you prefer.

TIP

I am told by the cooler members of my clan that wearing the belt clip is the modern equivalent of wearing a pocket protector.

Seidio also offers an attractive and effective solution, as seen in Figure 17-2.

You don't just use a good case so that you can hand off a clean used phone to the next lucky owner. A case makes it a little less likely that you will lose your phone. Your Galaxy S8 in its naked form is shiny glass and metal, which are slippery. Cases tend to have a higher coefficient of friction and prevent your phone from slipping out of your pocket when you take a ride in an Uber car.

More significantly, a case protects your phone against damage. If your phone is damaged, you have to mail it or bring it to a repair shop. The problem is that many people who bring their phones in for repair don't wipe the personal information off their devices. You really hope that the repair shop can pop off the broken piece, pop on a new one, and send you on your way. It's rarely that easy. Typically, you need to leave your phone in the hands of strangers for some period of time. For the duration of the repair, said strangers have access to the information on your phone.

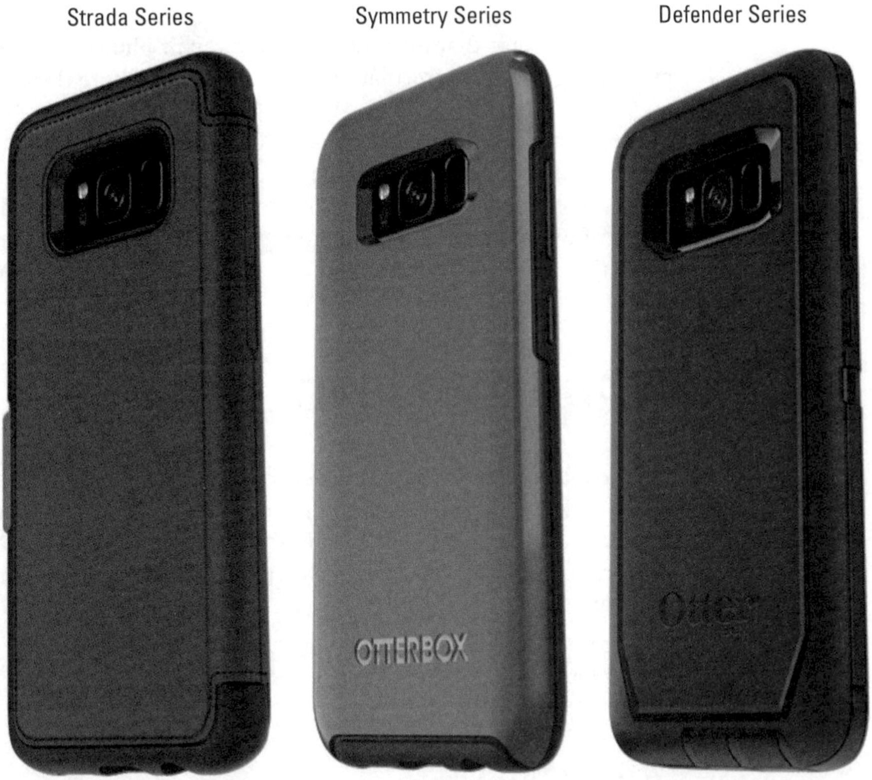

Strada Series   Symmetry Series   Defender Series

FIGURE 17-1:
Otterbox
cases for the
Samsung
Galaxy S8
and S8+.

FIGURE 17-2:
Seidio cases for
the Samsung
Galaxy S8
and S8+.

The good news is that most workers who repair phones are professional and will probably ignore any information from the phone before they start fixing it.

However, are you sure that you want to trust the professionalism of a stranger? Also, do you really want the hassle of getting a new phone? Probably not, so invest in a good case and screen cover. There are many options for different manufacturers of cases. Be sure to shop around to come up with the ideal combination of protection and style right for you.

Putting It on Lockdown

The most basic effort you can take to protect your phone is to put some kind of a screen lock on your phone. If you're connected to a corporate network, the company may have a policy that specifies what you must do to access your corporate network. Otherwise, you have eight choices, listed here in increasing degrees of security:

» Unlock with a simple swipe across the screen.

» Unlock with a pattern that you swipe on the screen.

» Unlock with a PIN.

» Unlock with facial recognition.

» Unlock with a password.

» Unlock with your fingerprint.

» Unlock with an iris scan.

» Encrypt the data on your SD card.

You can select any of the first seven of these options in the Lock Screen option in Settings. Encrypting everything on your phone (the last listed option) has some serious implications, so I describe it in more detail later in the chapter, in the "Encrypt Your SD Card" section.

If you want to choose one of the first six options, here's what you do:

1. **Tap the Settings icon.**

   This should be old hat by now.

2. **Tap the Lock Screen and Security link.**

   This brings up the options seen in Figure 17-3. You set some of the options mentioned in the preceding list and others when you follow the next instruction. This can be a little confusing, but bear with me while I explain your options and tell you where to go.

FIGURE 17-3:
The Lock
Screen and
Security
options.

3. **Tap the Screen Lock Type link.**

   This brings up the options seen in Figure 17-4. Each option prompts you through what it needs before establishing your security selection.

TIP

For reasons that sort of make sense, your phone uses some terminology that can be confusing. To clarify, the term *Screen Lock* is an option you can select to prevent unauthorized users from getting into your phone. The term *Lock Screen* is short for the action of locking your screen or enabling the Screen Lock option.

FIGURE 17-4:
The Screen
Lock options.

Preparing for your Screen Lock option

Regardless of what screen lock you choose, I recommend that you have ready the following choices at hand:

>> An unlock pattern

>> A PIN

>> A password

>> Your fingerprint

>> Your face

>> Your eyes

To clarify definitions, a *PIN* is a series of numbers. In this case, the PIN is four digits. A *password* is a series of numbers, upper- and lowercase letters, and sometimes special characters, and is typically longer than four characters. A PIN is pretty secure, but a password is usually more secure. Have them both ready, but decide which one you would prefer to use.

Selecting among the Screen Lock options

The first option, unlocking your phone with a swipe, fools exactly no one and doesn't slow anyone down. Rather than just having the Home screen appear, your phone tells you to swipe your finger on the screen to get to the Home screen. This is about as secure as waving at intruders and tossing them your phone, wallet, and keys. Let's keep going.

I recommend drawing out a pattern as the minimum screen-lock option. This is quick and easy. Tap the Pattern option on the screen seen in Figure 17-5 to get started. The phone asks you to enter your pattern and then asks you to enter it again. It then asks you to enter a PIN in case you forget your pattern.

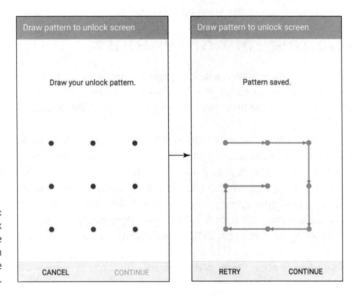

FIGURE 17-5: The unlock patterns: the blank screen and a sample pattern.

The unlock pattern is a design that you draw with your finger on a nine-dot screen, as shown in Figure 17-5.

The image on the right in Figure 17-5 happens to include all nine dots. You do not need to use all the dots. The minimum number of dots you must touch is four. The upper limit is nine because you can touch each dot only once. As long as you can remember your pattern, feel free to be creative.

TIP

Be sure to use a PIN you can remember a long time from now. You need this PIN only if you forget your pattern. That is a very rare situation for most people.

The next two options on the Screen Lock screen, PIN and Password, are more secure, but only as long as you avoid the obvious choices. If you insist upon using the PIN "0000" or "1111" or the word "password" as your password, don't waste your time. It's standard operating procedure within the typical den of thieves to try these sequences first. That's because so many people use these obvious choices.

WARNING

If, someday, you forget your pattern, your PIN, or your password, the only option is to do a complete reset of your phone back to original factory settings. In such a case, all your texts and stored files will be lost. Try to avoid this fate: Remember your pattern, PIN, or password.

Entering your fingerprints

Using your fingerprint to unlock your phone is very convenient. Once you have entered your, you can set it up so that you simply put your finger on the finger-print button, and your phone will open up to your home page.

There are a few hoops you need to make this happen. You need to give your phone enough views of the finger you will use, which can be whichever finger you like, so that it is sure that it is you. It also wants to make sure that you, and only you, have stored a fingerprint. Your phone can store multiple fingers, and you do not want to have any shenanigans going on here, like someone slipping in her fingerprint on to your phone. To prevent this from happening, you need to select a security option — again a pattern, PIN, or password — to access the fingerprint screen.

If you want to access your phone using a fingerprint, here's what you do:

1. **Tap on the Fingerprints link in the Screen Lock Type page (refer to Figure 17-4).**

   This will bring up the image seen in Figure 17-6.

2. **Enter your security selection for fingerprints.**

   This can be the same pattern, PIN, or password you used for the Home screen. Or not. The point is that this is to provide security to changing your fingerprint. When you have done this, the screen seen on the left of Figure 17-7 appears.

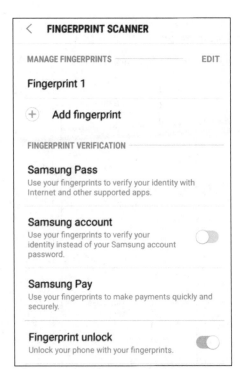

FIGURE 17-6:
The Fingerprint Security Options screen.

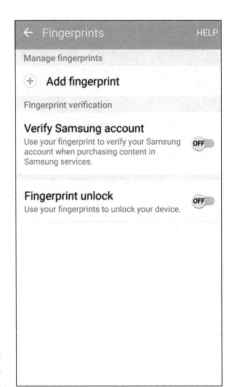

FIGURE 17-7:
The Fingerprints screen.

3. **Tap the Add Fingerprint option.**

   The leftmost screen in Figure 17-8 appears.

Start	In Process	Complete

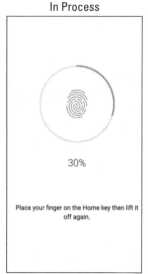 

FIGURE 17-8:
The Fingerprints
registration
screens.

4. **Press and hold lightly the Home button repeatedly.**

   Keep tapping the button in the rear of the phone until you reach 100 percent. The gray circle in the middle of Figure 17-8 will eventually turn completely blue, and then you get a congratulations screen on the right letting you know that you are at 100 percent.

   Enjoy this keen sense of accomplishment, because in a moment, you will be returned to a screen like the one shown in Figure 17-9. It is similar to Figure 17-6, but now has one stored fingerprint.

5. **Switch the Fingerprint unlock switch to the On position.**

Your fingerprint is now in memory and ready to let you get to your home page with a quick swipe. Give it a try. It is very slick!

Entering your face and/or iris

Facial recognition and the iris scan are even easier! From the Lockscreen and Security page, tap either Facial Recognition or Iris Scan. You'll be prompted to hold the phone toward your face. These recognition screens are shown in Figure 17-10. They work remarkably fast.

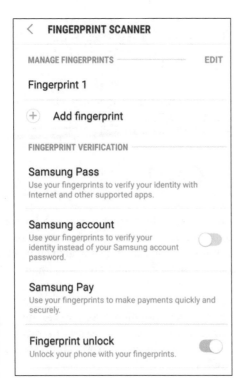

FIGURE 17-9:
The Fingerprints
screen with
one stored
fingerprint.

Face recognition Screen   Iris recognition Screen

FIGURE 17-10:
The facial
recognition
and iris scan
screens for
Mona Lisa.

The iris scan can struggle with contacts or glasses. Perhaps this can be your motivation to finally get Lasik eye surgery. Or, you can just use another, less convenient security method.

When your phone has your face or iris in its memory, all you need to do is hold up your phone when prompted, and it'll know that it's you!

Encrypting Your SD Card

This is the last Screen Lock option I list earlier in this section for protecting your device. It's an exceptionally secure option: It scrambles every file on your microSD card into gibberish, which it rapidly descrambles when you need the information. This sounds great; in practice, however, there are some important considerations to think about.

First, all this scrambling and descrambling takes processing power away from other things, such as running the apps. The loss is hardly noticeable in most cases — your phone is awash in processing power — but you never know when it may come back to bite you.

WARNING

After you encrypt your SD card, you can never switch it back to non-encrypted. With the Screen Lock options, you can use a PIN for a while, and then switch back to the pattern if you want, and live dangerously with the swipe option until you go to a password. Not so with the encryption option. You will never, ever, ever, ever get it back together.

If you encrypt your SD card and then forget your password, your SD card is toast. You won't be able to use these files ever again. Likewise, if you ever need to reset your phone to factory default settings, it won't remember how to talk to this SD card. Once again, toast is the word to describe the SD card and the data on it.

If you're sure that encryption is for you, here are the steps:

1. **From the Lock Screen and Security screen (refer to Figure 17-3), tap the Other Security Settings link.**

2. **Tap the Encrypt SD Card link.**

   Doing so brings up the warning screen, as shown in Figure 17-11.

   As the screen says, have your battery nicely charged, say, at 80 percent or higher, and an hour set aside when you don't need to use your phone.

3. **Tap the Encrypt SD Card option.**

   And off it goes. . . .

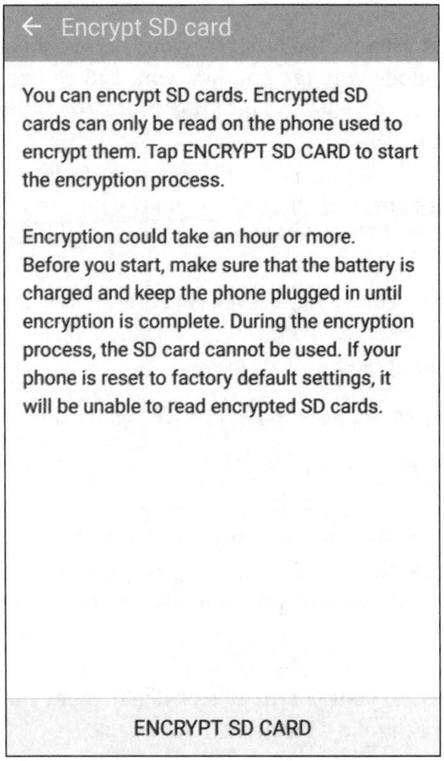

FIGURE 17-11:
The encryption
warning screen.

You can encrypt SD cards. Encrypted SD
cards can only be read on the phone used to
encrypt them. Tap ENCRYPT SD CARD to start
the encryption process.

Encryption could take an hour or more.
Before you start, make sure that the battery is
charged and keep the phone plugged in until
encryption is complete. During the encryption
process, the SD card cannot be used. If your
phone is reset to factory default settings, it
will be unable to read encrypted SD cards.

ENCRYPT SD CARD

Using Knox to Make Your Phone as Secure as Fort Knox

It doesn't matter whether you bought the phone at a retail store or your company supplied it to you. The fact of the matter is that company data that resides on your phone belongs to your employer. You probably signed a document (now sitting in your HR file) that states that you agree with this arrangement.

This policy is necessary for the company because it has a financial and legal obligation to protect company data, particularly if it pertains to individual customers. Like it or not, this obligation trumps your sense of privacy over the phone you bought and (still) pay for. If this really gets under your skin, you can always carry two smartphones: one for business and one for personal use. This solves the problem, but it's a hassle.

However, there is a better way. Samsung has a highly skilled group that has developed a secure system called *Knox.* Knox logically divides your phone into two modes: one for business use and the other for your personal use. You tap an icon, and you're in business mode. You tap another icon, and you're in personal mode. Switching between the two is instant, and Knox keeps the information from each mode separate.

TIP

This is a capability that is only of interest to you if your employer offers support for the service.

When it is available, Knox comes with three capabilities for the employer:

>> Security for the Android OS

>> Limitations on the applications that access the business side of your phone

>> Remote mobile-device management

This arrangement means that your employer can remotely control the business apps and potentially wipe the data on the business side at its discretion — but it has nothing to do with your personal information. The personal side remains your responsibility.

TIP

You may want to suggest to your company's IT department that it look into supporting Knox. Doing so can take a burden off your back.

Being Careful with Bluetooth

In Chapter 3, I looked at syncing your phone with Bluetooth devices. I did not mention the potential for security risk at that point. I do it now.

Some people are concerned that people with a radio scanner can listen in on their voice calls. This was possible, but not easy, in the early days of mobile phone use. Your Galaxy S8 can use only digital systems, so picking your conversation out of the air is practically impossible.

Some people are concerned that a radio scanner and a computer can pick up your data connection. It's not that simple. Maybe the NSA could get some of your data that way using complicated supercomputing algorithms, but it's much easier for thieves and pranksters to use wired communications to access the accounts of the folks who use "0000" as their PIN and "password" or "password1" as their password.

Perhaps the greatest vulnerability your phone faces is called *bluejacking*, which involves using some simple tricks to gain access to your phone via Bluetooth.

Do a test: The next time you're in a public place, such as a coffee shop, a restaurant, or a train station, turn on Bluetooth. Tap the button that makes you visible to all Bluetooth devices and then tap Scan. While your Bluetooth device is visible, you'll see all the other Bluetooth devices in your vicinity. You'll probably find lots of them. If not, try this at an airport. Wow!

If you were trying to pair with another Bluetooth device, you'd be prompted to see whether you're willing to accept connection to that device. In this case, you are not.

However, a hacker will see that you are open for pairing and take this opportunity to use the PIN 0000 to make a connection. When you're actively pairing, your Bluetooth device won't accept an unknown device's offer to pair. But if your device is both unpaired and visible, hackers can fool your Bluetooth device and force a connection.

After a connection is established, all your information is available to the hackers to use as they will. Here are the steps to protect yourself:

>> **Don't pair your phone to another Bluetooth device in a public place.**
Believe it or not, crooks go to public places to look for phones in pairing mode. When they pair with a phone, they look for interesting data to steal. It would be nice if these people had more productive hobbies, like Parkour or searching for Bigfoot. However, as long as these folks are out there, it is safer to pair your Bluetooth device in a not-so-public place.

>> **Make sure that you know the name of the device with which you want to pair.** You should pair only with that device. Decline if you are not sure or if other Bluetooth devices offer to connect.

>> **Shorten the default time-out setting.** The default is that you will be visible for two minutes. However, you can go into the menu settings and change the option for Visible Time-out to whatever you want. Make this time shorter than two minutes. *Don't set it to Never Time Out.* This is like leaving the windows open and the keys in the ignition on your Cadillac Escalade. A shorter time of visibility means that you have to be vigilant for less time.

>> **From time to time, check the names of the devices that are paired to your device.** If you don't recognize the name of a device, click the Settings icon to the right of the unfamiliar name and unpair it. Some damage may have been done by the intruder, but with any luck, you've nipped it in the bud.

Here's an important point: When handled properly, Bluetooth is as secure as can be. However, a few mistakes can open you up to human vermin with more technical knowledge than decency. Don't make those mistakes, and you can safely enjoy this capability, knowing that all the data on your phone is safe.

Protecting Against Malware

One of the main reasons application developers write apps for Android is that Google doesn't have an onerous preapproval process for a new app to be placed in the Play Store. This is unlike the Apple App Store or Microsoft Windows Phone Store, where each derivation of an app must be validated.

Many developers prefer to avoid bureaucracy. At least in theory, this attracts more developers to do more stuff for Android phones.

However, this approach does expose users like you and me to the potential for malware that can, inadvertently or intentionally, do things that are not advertised. Some of these "things" may be minor annoyances, or they could really mess up your phone (for openers).

Market forces, in the form of negative feedback, are present to kill apps that are badly written or are meant to steal your private data. However, this informal safeguard works only after some poor soul has experienced problems — such as theft of personal information — and reported it.

Rather than simply avoiding new apps, you can download apps designed to protect the information on your phone. These are available from many of the firms that make antivirus software for your PC. Importantly, many of these antivirus applications are free. If you want a nicer interface and some enhanced features, you can pay a few dollars, but it isn't necessary.

Examples include NG Mobile Security and Antivirus, Lookout Security and Antivirus, Kaspersky Mobile Security, and Norton Security Antivirus. If you have inadvertently downloaded an app that includes malicious software, these apps will stop that app.

Downloading Apps Only from Reputable Sources

Another way to avoid malware is to download mobile software only from trustworthy websites. This book has focused exclusively on the Google Play Store. You can download Android apps for your phone from a number of other reputable sites, including Amazon Appstore and GetJar.

Keep in mind that these stores are always on the lookout to withdraw applications that include malicious software. Google uses an internally developed solution it calls Bouncer to check for malicious software and remove it from the Play Store. Other mobile software distribution companies have their own approaches to addressing this problem. The problem is that policing malicious software is a hit-or-miss proposition.

As a rule, you should hesitate to download an Android application unless you know where it has been. You are safest if you restrict your app shopping to reputable companies. Be very skeptical of any other source of an Android application.

Rescuing Your Phone When It Gets Lost

Other options allow you to be more proactive than waiting for a Good Samaritan to reach out to your home phone or email if you lose your phone.

There are apps that help you find your phone. Here are a few several "lost it" scenarios and some possible solutions for your quandary:

>> **You know that you lost your phone somewhere in your house. You would try calling your own number, but you had your phone set to Vibrate Only mode.**

Solution: Remote Ring. By sending a text to your phone with the "right" code that you preprogrammed when you set up this service, your phone will ring on its loudest setting, even if you have the ringer set to Vibrate Only.

If you know that your phone is in your house, the accuracy of GPS isn't savvy enough to tell you whether it's lost between the seat cushions of your couch or in the pocket of your raincoat. That's where the Remote Ring feature comes in handy.

>> **You lost your phone while traveling and have no idea whether you left it in a taxi or at airport security.**

Solution: Map Current Location. This feature allows you to track, within the accuracy of the GPS signal, the location of your phone. You need access to the website of the company with which you arranged to provide this service, and it will show you (on a map) the rough location of your phone.

Here is where having an account with Samsung comes in handy. Hopefully, you signed up for a Samsung Account when you first got your phone. If you did, you're signed up for the Find My Mobile at `http://findmymobile.samsung.com`. Figure 17-12 shows the Find My Mobile PC screen.

FIGURE 17-12: The Samsung Find My Mobile PC screen.

All you need to do is get to a PC and sign in to your Samsung account. You can tell your phone to ring by clicking on Ring my device. You can have the PC bring up a map by clicking Locate My Device.

I suggest trying these out before you lose your phone the first time.

Wiping Your Device Clean

As a last-ditch option, you can use Find My Mobile (see preceding section) to remotely disable your device or wipe it clean. Here are some of the possible scenarios:

>> **You were robbed, and a thief has your phone.**

Solution: Remote Lock. After your phone has been taken, this app allows you to create a four-digit PIN that, when sent to your phone from another mobile phone or a web page, locks down your phone. This capability is above and beyond the protection you get from your Screen Lock and prevents further access to applications, phone, and data.

WARNING

If you know that your phone was stolen — that is, not just lost — do *not* try to track down the thief yourself. Get the police involved and let them know that you have this service on your phone — and that you know where your phone is.

>> **You're a very important executive or international spy. You stored important plans on your phone, and you have reason to believe that the "other side" has stolen your phone to acquire your secrets.**

Solution: Remote Erase. Also known as Remote Wipe, this option resets the phone to its factory settings, wiping out all the information and settings on your phone.

TIP

You can't add Remote Erase *after* you've lost your phone. You must sign up for your Samsung service beforehand. It's not possible to remotely enable this capability to your phone. You need to have your phone in hand when you download and install either a lock app or a wipe app.

Index

Symbols and Numerics

About the Author

Bill Hughes is an experienced marketing strategy executive with over two decades of experience in sales, strategic marketing, and business development roles at several leading corporations, including Xerox, Microsoft, IBM, General Electric, Motorola, and US West Cellular.

Bill has worked with Microsoft to enhance its marketing to mobile applications developers. He also has led initiatives to develop new products and solutions with several high-tech organizations, including Sprint Nextel, Motorola, SBC, and Tyco Electronics.

Bill was a professor of marketing at the Kellogg School of Management at Northwestern University, where he taught Business Marketing to graduate MBA students.

Bill also has written articles on wireless technology for several wireless industry trade magazines. He also has contributed to articles in *USA Today* and *Forbes*. These articles were based upon his research reports written for In-Stat, where he was a principal analyst, covering the wireless industry, specializing in smartphones and business applications of wireless devices.

Bill graduated with honors with an MBA degree from the Kellogg School of Management at Northwestern University and earned a Bachelor of Science degree with distinction from the College of Engineering at Cornell University, where he was elected to the Tau Beta Pi Engineering Honorary.

Dedication

I would like to dedicate this book to Lindsey Smith.

Author's Acknowledgments

I need to thank a number of people who helped make this book a reality. First, I would like thank my literary agent, Carole Jelen, of Waterside Publishing, for her support, encouragement, knowledge, and negotiation skills.

I would also like to thank the team at Wiley Publishing: Katie Mohr and Elizabeth Kuball. Your expertise helped me through the creative process. Thanks for your guidance.

I would like to thank Philip Berne of Samsung Electronics America for his ongoing assistance. Philip's help was critical in producing this book.

I would also like to thank Kristen Tatti of Otterbox, Bristol Whitcher of TYLT, Hari Seedhar of Soen Audio, and Summer Su of CRAZY BABY.

I would like to acknowledge Ellis, Arlen, Quinlan, and Indy, for trying to keep me grounded (using the positive definition of the word). I would like to thank Lindsey Smith for keeping Ellis semi-grounded.

WITHDRAWN

Publisher's Acknowledgments

Executive Editor: Katie Mohr
Project Editor: Elizabeth Kuball
Copy Editor: Elizabeth Kuball
Sr. Editorial Assistant: Cherie Case

Production Editor: Selvakumaran Rajendiran
Cover Image: © Floriana/iStockphoto

11-28-17
$24.99

LONGWOOD PUBLIC LIBRARY
800 Middle Country Road
Middle Island, NY 11953
(631) 924-6400
longwoodlibrary.org

LIBRARY HOURS

Monday-Friday	9:30 a.m. - 9:00 p.m.
Saturday	9:30 a.m. - 5:00 p.m.
Sunday (Sept-June)	1:00 p.m. - 5:00 p.m.